World Textiles

A Sourcebook

World Textiles

A Sourcebook

THE BRITISH MUSEUM PRESS

© 2012 The Trustees of the British Museum

First published in 2012 by The British Museum Press
A division of The British Museum Company Ltd
38 Russell Square, London WC1B 3QQ

www.britishmuseum.org/publishing

A catalogue record for this book is available from
the British Library

ISBN: 978-0-7141-5093-2

Designer: Grade Design
Maps: Olive Pearson (pp. 26, 32, 38, 44, 56, 62)
and Technical Art Services (pp. 8, 14, 20, 50)
Printed by C&C Offset, China

The content of this book is drawn from material previously
published in the The British Museum Press *Fabric Folios* series:

Textiles from the Balkans Diane Waller
Embroidery from Palestine Shelagh Weir
Embroidery from Afghanistan Sheila Paine
Embroidery from India and Pakistan Sheila Paine
Miao Textiles from China Gina Corrigan
Textiles from Guatemala Ann Hecht
Textiles from Mexico Chloë Sayer
Textiles from the Andes Penelope Dransart and Helen Wolfe
Silk in Africa Chris Spring and Julie Hudson
Printed and Dyed Textiles from Africa John Gillow

The introduction (pp. 6–69) was abridged and edited from the
original *Fabric Folio* introductions by Chloë Sayer. The text on
pp. 51–5 was also written by Chloë.

The textiles featured in this book are from the collection of the
British Museum and have been selected from the viewpoint of
their design. The British Museum registration numbers for these
textiles are listed on pp. 362–3. To find out more about these
and objects in all areas of the British Museum's collection, visit
www.britishmuseum.org

The picture credits for the contextual photographs featured in
the introduction are given on p. 359.

Frontispiece Detail of a woman's pleated apron worked in
coloured wools. Bulgaria, nineteenth century. 87 x 58 cm
(34 x 23 in). Donated by Mrs Protitch Moreggio.

Opposite Pompom detail on a woman's apron. See p. 100
for full caption.

Contents

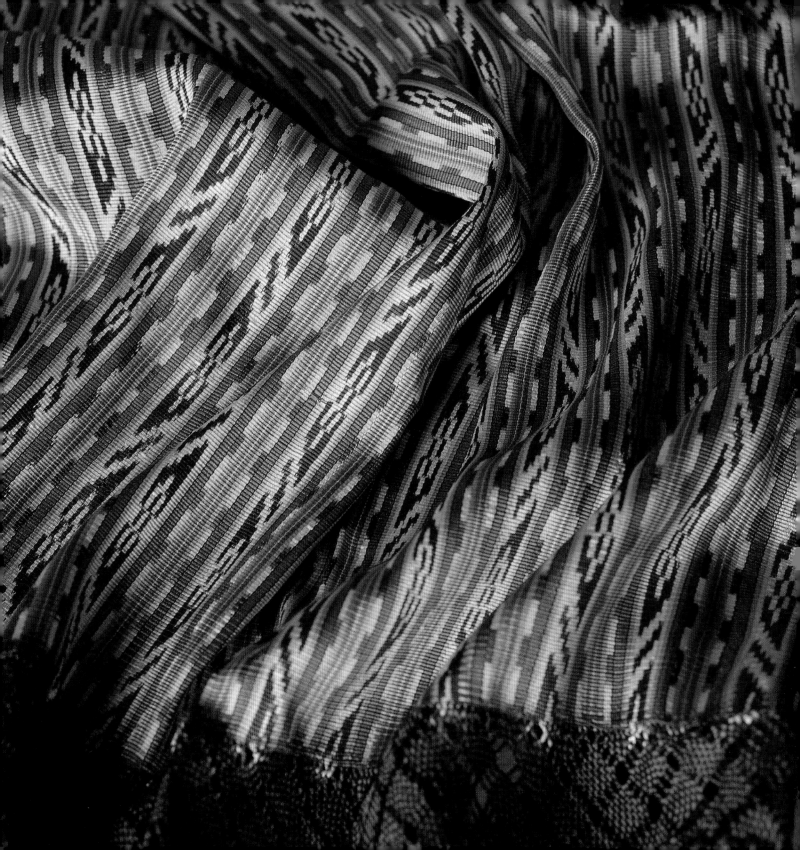

introduction

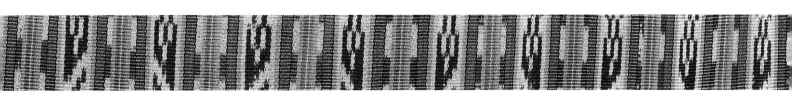

Textiles have a long and enduring history. For centuries they have played an important role in the everyday lives of people all over the world. Textiles are practical but for many they also have a strong ritualistic and ceremonial significance – in weddings, festivals and feast day celebrations. They are also an expression of identity and status: a woman's clothing, for instance, could reveal not only where she was from (right down to the specific village) but also whether she was married, looking for a husband or in mourning. Rich with cultural meaning and often bearing religious or spiritual significance, these textiles tell us much about the skills and lives of the people who made and wore them.

The introduction here provides an overview of the textile traditions and techniques in countries and regions around the world renowned for their textile heritage, considering them within the context of the lives and environments of their makers and wearers. The selection of textiles that follows (taken from the fine collection of the British Museum) is intended to provide inspiration for using pattern and colour and so the textiles featured have been chosen from the viewpoint of their design.

TEXTILES FROM THE BALKANS

The Balkans are a complex mosaic of ethnic, religious and cultural groups, each with distinct traditions that cross national frontiers. Although the region takes its name from the Balkan Mountains, which run through the centre of Bulgaria into eastern Serbia, it now covers a broader geographical area and takes in many countries in south-eastern Europe. Baking summers and freezing winters, combined with poor-quality land, have made existence difficult for people of the Balkans, yet their cultural heritage is rich and diverse. Dances, music, folk customs and clothing styles have been influenced by the Slavs, Thracians, Proto-Bulgarians and Greeks of antiquity and the Middle Ages. Part of the Ottoman Empire for 500 years, the Balkans have also absorbed Ottoman and Islamic influences (the Turks only relinquished control of Macedonia in 1912).

The selection featured in this book includes textiles from Albania, Greece, Bulgaria and the former Yugoslavia (in particular the region of Macedonia) and most were made during the first half of the twentieth century. Some bear the stains of daily labour in house, yard and field, and tell us much about the lives of the women and men who wore them. Others were made for weddings, festivals and feast days, which offered light relief from harsh living conditions. But traditional clothing has been subjected to change. Except in remote areas of the Balkans, traditional clothing is no longer considered suitable for everyday wear. Rapid industrialization over the past forty years has promoted the spread of Western-style clothing. Many families have sold their costumes and although textiles are still produced – often for local dance groups and tourists – older, handmade costumes are increasingly seen only in museums or on the stage at folk-dance festivals.

TECHNIQUES

Before industrialization, weaving was a basic skill throughout the Balkans. Woven goods, widely traded and exported, were made on horizontal looms from hemp, linen and wool, with cotton used more recently, and occasionally silk. Bulgaria's Chiprovtsi region is famous for its *kilims* (flat woven carpets). Households traditionally wove rugs, *kilims* and other items for daily use, and decorated the home for special occasions such as births, weddings and funerals. In Greece, during the eighteenth century, weaving developed into an organized industry in which men also took part.

Balkan embroidery has absorbed influences from Byzantium and from medieval, Renaissance and Ottoman traditions. Most embroiderers worked by counting the threads of the fabric: the most popular stitches were cross, oblique, straight, split and knotted. Materials included linen, cotton and wool. Silk was used in those regions where the silkworm was bred and was a valuable export.

DESIGN, PATTERN AND COLOUR

Balkan designs include the ancient rhomb (diamond shape), simple or complicated geometrical forms, and hook-shaped motifs. Some textiles also incorporate flowers and other plant motifs, animals, birds and insects. Under Turkish influence, *kilims* were made which featured similar patterns and colours: birds, animals and plants – particularly the 'tree of life' motif, which takes the form of a flower-filled receptacle, flanked by animal or human figures.

Vegetable dyes produced subtle shades of dark blue, brown, dark red and green. Albanian *kilim*-weavers in Kosovo also used black, dark brown, violet and yellow. After the introduction of chemical dyes in the nineteenth century, colours became cruder and brighter; *pembe* ('shocking pink') proved especially popular among the local population. Although *kilims* are still produced today, most bear little resemblance to the finely crafted examples of earlier times.

CLOTHING STYLES

Underlying all Balkan costume is a complex belief system that dictated the type of garment and the decoration. Women's clothing styles were extremely diverse. They indicated the age and social status of wearers and identified their village or town. As women grew older, the colours and variety of costume diminished. The chemise – the undergarment for most costumes – was made from flax that had been washed, beaten and bleached in sunlight. The chemise or dress was heavily embroidered at the openings – the neck, sleeves and hem – to protect against the entry of evil spirits. Over the chemise, women wore a variety of different jackets or overdresses made of wool, linen or padded cotton.

Jackets were usually decorated with couched braid or embroidered down the front and on the back and hem, sometimes with gold or silver metal-wrapped thread and with fur and velvet around the cuffs. Women either wore a single apron, wrapped round the lower half of the body, or two aprons, one often pleated at the back and the other straight at the front. Aprons, like embroidery, were thought to protect the body from evil spirits; this explains why they were worn front and back. Woollen aprons, of varying thicknesses, were strikingly patterned with geometric motifs and stripes. In another variety of costume, a sleeveless overdress of dark blue or black woollen material was worn over the chemise; because it was knee-length, it revealed the embroidery on the bottom of the chemise.

After 1900 the ever-increasing range and availability of fabrics, braids and ornaments led women to add decorations to the basic embroidery. Costumes, passed down from grandmother to granddaughter, often underwent change as lace or crochet, ribbons, sequins and beads were added in an attempt to personalize designs. Despite such amendments, however, the basic form of women's costume remained the same in the regions mentioned here. The often elaborate appearance of clothing bore no relation to the economic circumstances of the wearer. In order to keep daughters 'correctly' dressed and to avoid the scorn of neighbours, impoverished families were prepared to incur large debts and even to sell land.

In Greece there were three categories of costume. The hand-woven village category was typified by cotton chemises worn with pinafore dresses and woollen coats. These same elements, but made from more expensive materials, were required for the urban category seen in Yanina

Women from Kotel, central Bulgaria at a festival.

(Joánnina) – this style survived in Greek communities in Asia Minor until the early twentieth century. Wearers of the more modern Western urban category used a long pleated dress of expensive silk cloth over a cotton chemise; an embroidered woollen jacket or a felt waistcoat, embroidered with fine gold braid, was worn as a topcoat. The naturalistic elements of Greek embroidery, influenced initially by Persian traditions, centre on the 'tree of life' motif. Other elements from Greek life and tradition – the snake, cock, double-headed eagle, mermaid, wedding scene, betrothal, bridal pair, musicians and dancers – were also common.

In areas of Serbia, Montenegro and Bulgaria where Western European fashions held sway, town costumes were made from expensive materials such as fine quality wool imported from Central Europe. In nineteenth-century Serbia, Kosovo and parts of Bulgaria urban clothing was usually made from silk, velvet and fine linen.

Embroidery was done with silk or gold and silver thread. Fur-trimmed jackets and other costume elements were often made by tailors.

In Macedonia, early Balkan people, the ancient Greeks, Romans and medieval civilizations have left a rich legacy. These diverse influences are reflected in the region's designs and textile styles. Embroidery from the region of Galičnik in the Former Yugoslavia Republic of Macedonia, is especially fine: predominately red, with small elements of yellow, it features pulled or drawn threadwork. Costumes are multilayered, with unmarried women wearing a simpler woollen overjacket pleated at the back. Jackets are typically embellished with a multitude of gold filigree buttons.

Embroiderers in Macedonia often incorporate a flower motif associated with the historic battle of 1389, when the Turks defeated the Serbs on the plains of Kosovo. Legend has it that thousands of peonies grew up from the blood of slain warriors. The embroidered red hues symbolize bloodshed, while the dark colours framing the red represent the nation's sorrow at losing its freedom.

People in rural communities across the Balkans wore leather shoes: made from a single piece of leather, they were shaped like moccasins. Hand-knitted socks, plain and patterned, were used by men and women. Designs included

A young woman at St Lazarus's day festival, Sliven, Lazarka, Bulgaria.

was important everywhere and was part of a bride's dowry.

Male outfits were simpler than those worn by women. Most men used a shirt embroidered at the neck, down the front and on the cuffs, thick baggy woollen trousers, a woven sash, jackets and woollen socks. In northern Bulgaria men wore boots or clogs rather than leather shoes. In parts of Macedonia and Greece, as in the Pirin region of Bulgaria, men wore a knee-length white linen chemise over white linen or wool trousers, with a tightly wrapped sash over the chemise giving the impression of a skirt. In the mountainous Marievo region of Macedonia, a pleated apron-skirt was worn over thick woollen trousers and richly patterned socks.

In towns clothing was more elaborate: rich merchants, who copied the customs of the ruling power, donned jackets thickly trimmed with fur and embroidered in silver and gold thread, and cloaks of brocade and velvet. In winter, in the countryside men wore heavy sheepskin coats, woollen cloaks and hats of fur or sheepskin. Shepherds used heavy cloaks with pointed hoods. In Kosovo – even in summer – many Albanian men still wear their thick felted wool costumes and white felted hats.

THE ROLE OF CLOTHING IN CEREMONY

Many Balkan textiles were made for festive and ceremonial occasions: they marked the rites of passage, from birth through to death, that punctuated people's lives. When babies were christened, they wore little caps decorated with

geometric forms, flowers, animals, birds and insects. Knitters, working with five needles, decorated just the visible areas – when given as presents, however, socks were decorated in their entirety.

Each costume had its own headgear, ranging from a simple scarf to ornate silver and coin caps, or constructions of flowers, feathers and beads for special occasions. Heavy jewellery, often of silver, red threads and coins. A key duty of the godfather was to provide the child's first proper clothes and wrappings. When babies began to crawl, added to their basic shirt would be leggings, a woollen kilt-like garment, and a little coat. This was the usual form of dress for boys and girls until the age of three, and sometimes even until six or seven. They then progressed to wearing a little dress with a gathered skirt under their shirts, or a longish shirt and a waistcoat.

After reaching puberty, when a girl put on full folk costume for the first time – perhaps during one of the major spring festivals – she was allowed to join the village dances. Her outfit, made with her own hands, displayed her skill and maturity, and indicated that she was ready for betrothal. When a boy came of age, he would don an embroidered shirt and braided trousers with a long woollen sash. He could now take part in village dances and look for a bride. Often contact was established at a *sedyanka*. In an era when boys and girls were strictly segregated, this was an autumn or winter gathering where young people could socialize. Girls would wear their best clothing and spin or embroider. Boys would play music, tell stories and join in the dancing. In many villages in the Balkans, aspects of the *sedyanka* are still followed.

Domestic skills were seen as crucially important in a future bride. Each girl prepared her own trousseau. This was a huge undertaking, comprising several sets of clothing, household goods, numerous socks, aprons and shirts, as well as towels to be presented to guests at the wedding. In Macedonia splendid wedding outfits were worn by the women of Galičnik and by the Sarakatsan (a nomadic people of Greek origin). Sarakatsan costumes are predominantly dark red, blue and black, with heavy pleated skirts and luxuriously decorated jackets and aprons. Muslim wedding costumes in Serbia were richly decorated with a predominance of gold. Brides everywhere were expected to wear as much jewellery as possible. In some areas custom required the bride to stand throughout her wedding day and the following night (during which time the bridegroom slept) wearing the heavy costume and jewellery that formed part of her dowry.

Weddings and the preparations that preceded them involved elaborate rituals. Across the various regions marriages were vitally important events, because economic stability depended on the prosperous union of families. Many wedding festivities lasted an entire week, with traditional songs, music and dances. Sometimes rituals continued after marriage. In parts of the former Yugoslavia, for example, women wore their bridal attire every Sunday until the birth of the first child.

The textiles on pp. 70–101 show enormous skill and creativity, and convey the cultural complexity of the Balkans. They belong to a bygone age, destroyed by industrialization and by the traumatic events of war in the twentieth century.

Countries of the eastern Mediterranean 2011

TURKEY

CYPRUS

SYRIA

LEBANON

Golan
Heights

Gaza Strip

West
Bank

ISRAEL

EGYPT

JORDAN

SAUDI

ARABIA

Eilat
Aqaba

LEBANON

Lake
Huleh

Acre

Safed

SYRIA

GALILEE

Lake
Tiberias

Haifa

Tiberias

Nazareth

Beisan

Jenin

Tulkarm

TRANSJORDAN

Nablus

Qalqilya

River Jordan

Tel Aviv
Jaffa

Beit Dajan

Lydda

Bir Zeit

Ramleh

Ramallah

Jericho

MEDITERRANEAN SEA

Ashdod

Jerusalem

Beit Jala

Mejdel

Bethlehem

Falujeh

Hebron

Dead Sea

Gaza

Khan Yunis

0   20   40 km

Rafah

Beersheba

EGYPT

NEGEV DESERT

EMBROIDERY FROM PALESTINE

We do not know when the village women of Palestine began to adorn their garments with embroidery and patchwork. However, textiles collected by Christian missionaries and travellers, and preserved in European museums, show that embroidery was already a highly developed art by the mid-nineteenth century. The beautiful textiles featured here were made by Arab women between the early nineteenth century and the mid-twentieth century. This period includes the last of four centuries of Ottoman rule, which ended after the First World War, and the three decades of British Mandate rule beginning in 1918 and ending with the establishment of the State of Israel in northern, western and southern Palestine in 1948. During this time, the population of Palestine was – as it had been for centuries – predominantly Arab and Muslim, with a minority of Christian Arabs and Jews. The majority of the Arabs lived in over eight hundred agricultural villages scattered throughout the coastal plain and in the hills to the north and east. The rest lived in towns and generally followed the fashions of the Turkish or British ruling classes. The remainder of the Palestinian Arabs were nomadic or semi-nomadic Bedouin who lived in the deserts and relied mainly on animal-herding. Only village embroidery is considered here.

ORIGINS AND INFLUENCES

Palestinian costume and embroidery were subject to diverse influences. Major trade and travel routes passed through Palestine, connecting it to neighbouring countries of the eastern Mediterranean, and further afield. Enticing textiles, mainly from Syria, Turkey and Europe, found their way into the markets of the main towns. Many foreigners went to Palestine as tourists or officials, or as pilgrims to its Muslim, Christian or Jewish holy places, all wearing their own traditional costumes or with cloth or clothing to sell. Christian missionaries from England, Germany and America, who ran embroidery classes and commissioned work from local women, also introduced new designs. From the 1930s, the marketing of European materials and pattern books markedly influenced local styles. Women were also surrounded by indigenous sources of artistic inspiration: architectural ornaments; oriental rugs displayed in markets; the uniforms of Ottoman and British officials; and the ornate vestments of the Christian clergy. While the village women of Palestine borrowed ideas from all such sources, however, their art was fundamentally sustained by their own customs and values.

A FEMALE ART

Embroidery was (and remains) an exclusively female art. Techniques and patterns were passed down from generation to generation. As soon as a girl was old enough to wield a needle – around the age of six – she was given a scrap of cloth, a few threads to practise with and embroidery to copy. This was considered an important educational process which involved learning both a physical skill and a complex system of visual communication. Every stitch and motif had a name. Each garment also had an embroidery structure, and patterns had to be combined in particular ways according to the customs of each village at different periods. Styles were never static. Fashions changed as new ideas were introduced and copied by others.

Once a girl became competent at sewing, she began preparing articles for her wedding trousseau: unadorned dresses and veils for everyday working life, and richly embroidered garments for special occasions and festivities. Her father or guardian paid for these, and provided her silver dowry jewellery – considered her share of the 'brideprice' paid by the groom. The groom contributed luxury items bought from textile merchants and professionally embroidered panels or garments. The preparation of the trousseau took many months – sometimes years. Embroidery silks were expensive so were bought piecemeal as families could afford them. Embroidery was done on pieces of fabric which were later sewn together to make complete garments.

Girls wore their trousseau garments for the first time at their weddings. Ceremonies typically lasted a week and culminated with a procession welcoming the bride back into society after her period of ritual seclusion, and celebrating her transformation from unmarried virgin to married woman. For this flamboyant and exclusively female event, the new bride donned her finest dress and all her silver dowry jewellery.

Woman embroidering in a refugee camp, Amman, Jordan, 1987. She is using mercerized cotton thread, and waste canvas on a synthetic fabric.

Thereafter her trousseau was kept for special occasions. After marriage, women embroidered new ceremonial garments to replace those which wore out or became unfashionable. A few with the talent and time sometimes took up dressmaking and embroidery professionally.

FABRIC AND DYES

Women's everyday garments were made from handwoven cotton or linen. These fabrics were left their natural colour, or indigo-dyed different shades of blue. (The darkest were the most expensive, because it took several dye baths to achieve deep shades.) The open weave of the cloth enabled embroiderers to plan their overall designs and individual motifs by counting threads. This was particularly important for cross stitch, the main stitch of southern Palestine.

Garments were not tailored or shaped to the body. The pieces for everyday garments were sewn together, edge to edge, with simple running, zigzag or herringbone stitches. Dresses and coats were reinforced with facings inside openings, and with shoulder and chest patches to prevent wear by silver ornaments. They were also reinforced around hems to prevent them fraying when they brushed the ground. Decorative embroidery and appliqué probably evolved from this functional stitching and protective patchwork or binding.

Festive garments were either made from the same plain cottons and linens as everyday dresses, or from finer fabrics containing silk yarn. These fabrics were made in weaving centres in Palestine, or imported from Syria. The floss silk used in embroidery came from Mount Lebanon or from imported cocoons, and was dyed with kermes compounds to give shades of red, orange and yellow. Aniline-dyed silks were introduced into Syria and Palestine in the late nineteenth or early twentieth centuries, when small touches of brilliant pinks and greens began to appear among the predominant reds of Palestinian embroidery. They were widely adopted from the 1920s, eventually supplanting silks coloured with natural dyes. From the 1930s floss silks, with their lustrous sheen and subtle gradations of colour,

were superseded by *perlé* (mercerized) cotton threads made by the French company Dolfus Mieg et Cie (DMC), which came in a wide range of uniform shades. The introduction of embroidery canvas made it easier to embroider on imported fabrics with tight weaves, and encouraged a wider use of velvets, rayons and other synthetics. Women also copied new motifs from the pattern books marketed with the new threads.

SYMBOLISM AND STYLES

The specific patterns and colours of embroidery and appliqué proclaimed key aspects of a married woman's social identity – the area and even village she came from, and her wealth, age and marital status. Abundant garments with lavish decoration flaunted wealth. The predominantly red embroidery – symbolically associated with virginity, menstruation and childbirth – reflected the fact that women were of prime childbearing age; when they reached the menopause their embroidery became more restrained. Bright, rich embroidery was also an expression of normality and joy and was covered, turned inside out or dyed blue during periods of mourning.

Two major regional styles of dress and ornamentation developed in Palestine: that of the Galilee hills in northern Palestine, and that of southern Palestine. In Galilee women wore a short-sleeved, calf-length coat of indigo blue or russet-coloured cotton over a white tunic and ankle-length white or blue cotton trousers. Around their waists they wound patterned girdles, and on their heads they wore coin-encrusted bonnets covered by dark silk veils, or later, scarves bound with brocade headbands. Coats prepared for the trousseau and for special occasions were heavily embellished, from waist to hem, with stitched embroidery and patchwork. Trouser legs were also embroidered. Women used a wide range of stitches: satin stitch, running stitch, cross stitch, hem stitch and drawn threadwork. Embroidery was predominantly red with touches of other colours. Geometric motifs included diamonds, triangles, rectangles and chevrons; some coats were also ornamented with small floral motifs. Additional decoration was provided by appliquéd patches of red, green and yellow taffeta, or by sections of brilliantly coloured striped or *ikat*-patterned satin. These garments, apparently worn throughout Galilee during the first half of the nineteenth century, were gradually replaced by Turkish-style garments made from Syrian cottons and satins, and by the early twentieth century had gone out of fashion. Now it is impossible to delineate the main regional styles of costume that once existed in Galilee, or to understand their symbolism.

We know more about the traditional costumes of southern Palestine because they continued to be worn, in various transformations, throughout the twentieth century and into the twenty-first. There women wore long-sleeved, ankle-length dresses of dark-blue cotton or linen bound with sashes similar to those of Galilee. In some villages, these co-existed with white linen dresses. Heads were covered with flowing white veils which were draped over bonnets sewn with dowry coins. In south-west Palestine some dresses were made from a distinctive, locally woven navy-blue cotton with magenta or green silk stripes at the selvedge. A kind of coat-dress with short sleeves and an opening from waist to hem was worn in some areas, until it went out of fashion in the 1920s.

Southern Palestinian dresses were embroidered in symmetrical panels on the chest, sleeves, sides and lower back, according to the style of each region and group of villages. The embroidery on veils was either distributed in narrow bands along the edges, or in large motifs on the main body of the veil. Bonnets and cushion covers were likewise embroidered in different ways depending on area. As in Galilee, embroidery was predominantly red, enlivened with touches of other colours. The main stitch for creating patterns was cross stitch. Herringbone, satin stitch and running stitch were used for binding hems, joining seams and attaching decorative panels or patches of taffeta or satin. Embroidery patterns from the nineteenth and early twentieth centuries are mainly geometric, but from the 1930s these were increasingly replaced by representational motifs – such as birds and flowers – copied from pattern books.

The strikingly different embroidery technique of couching, adopted in and around Bethlehem before the mid-nineteenth century, was influenced by the cord and frogging which decorated the uniforms of Ottoman officials and soldiers, and by the flamboyant embroidery on church vestments. Couching, like appliqué, was a commercial enterprise. In many villages in southern Palestine, the groom was expected to provide his future bride with panels of couched embroidery. These were commissioned from specialists in the Bethlehem area, and from the 1920s also in the Jaffa area. Couching was executed in silk, gilt or silver cord. The principal garments embroidered with couching were dresses, jackets (worn only in the cool hills), and the distinctive fèz-shaped hats of Bethlehem.

EMBROIDERY NOW

During the hostilities surrounding the establishment of the state of Israel in 1948, an estimated three quarters of a million villagers fled or were driven from their homes in the Galilee hills or on the coastal plain. A second wave of refugees was created by the Six Day War of 1967. Most have since lived in refugee camps or towns in the Gaza Strip, the West Bank, Lebanon, Syria, Jordan or Egypt. Those who remained form a large minority within the Jewish state. These hardships and dislocations have affected every aspect of Palestinian life and culture, including dress. The worsening Palestinian economy under Israeli occupation has made embroidery difficult to afford during the early twenty-first century.

Many women of village origin now wear Western fashions or variations of unadorned 'Islamic' dress. The art and language of embroidery have nevertheless persisted, though

Woman in Ramallah, 1979. Her chest square is decorated with cross-stitch embroidery and gilt-cord couching, and her sleeves have taffeta inset panels with couched cuffs.

on a reduced scale, in the West Bank, Gaza Strip and Jordan, partly due to the efforts of income-generating projects organized by welfare associations. Although fashions in dress and embroidery have greatly changed, certain elements still indicate the wearer's place of origin in Palestine – even among refugees who left their villages decades ago, or those who have lived all their lives in exile. Such is the human desire for identity and homeland.

ARAL
SEA

U Z B E K I S T A N

Amu Darya River

T U R K M E N I S T A N

Repetek
desert

TAJIKISTAN   Pamir

Balkh
Mazar-i-Sharif   Kunduz

Hindu Kush   Kalash
Valleys

Herat   Bamiyan   NURISTAN

WARDAK   Kabul

AFGHANISTAN   Jalalabad

ORUZGAN   PAKTYA   Peshawar
              Ghazni

PAKTIKA

IRAN   Kandahar

                Quetta

P A K I S T A N

BALUCHISTAN

◆ national capital
● city / town

EMBROIDERY FROM AFGHANISTAN

The traditional embroidery of Afghanistan was an integral part of its tribal life: village women flashing vivid cuffs as their hands steadied loads of firewood; bicycle saddle covers couched with gold or bright with flowers; young men in the bazaar, their shirt fronts patterned in fine geometric grids. Each image was shot with colour and stitch. That image then changes to the abiding one of a young woman taking refuge in the wrecked airport of Kandahar – tracer bullets, bombs and rockets exploding around her – sitting calmly embroidering.

Embroidery must be considered within the context of the lives and environment of the people who make it. That context in Afghanistan has for many years been war. The Taliban movement, which began near Kandahar in 1994 with the aim of creating a pure Islamic state, made it illegal for women and girls to attend school, to sing, to listen to the radio, or to work. Embroidery played an even bigger role in the lives of these confined women and girls. Today many have become providers: embroidery, often their only means of support, represents survival.

Afghanistan's landlocked landscape is fractured into remote high valleys and formidable terrain, with the plains of the north largely cut off from the rest of the country. The isolation of much of its population has led to a great diversity of customs and traditions; paradoxically, as a strategically important region of transit and conquest, many areas have also been subjected to outside influences. It is significant that all the tribes, with the exception of the Hazara, also live outside the territory of Afghanistan. Within the country, the various ethnic groups tend to be concentrated in particular areas, although war, flight and migration to the cities have dramatically changed the population. In 1980 it numbered around fifteen million, of which by 1990 some five million at least had fled. By 2005, with the subjugation of the Taliban and the ensuing relative stability, more than two million had returned, though many refugees remain in Pakistan and Iran by choice.

THE TRIBES

The biggest ethnic group are the Pashtun. They are spread over much of the country, although most have settled in the south and east. More than twelve million live in Pakistan. The Tajik of the north-east number around three and a half million, while in Tajikistan there are six million. (The Tajik, like the Pashtun and most of the population of Afghanistan, are Sunnis.)

The Uzbek of the north are cut off from much of Afghanistan by the mountains of the Hindu Kush. Most live around Mazar-i-Sharif and Kunduz, while the Lakai Uzbek have settled near Balkh. They are people of Turko-Mongol origin who migrated to Afghanistan as Tsarist Russia and then the Soviets took over power in Uzbekistan. The Turkmen of the north live along the border with Turkmenistan, south-west of the Amu Darya river.

The Baluch of the south live in Baluchistan

and in Iran, while many of the Nuristanis of the north fled across the mountains to the Kalash valleys in northern Pakistan in the late nineteenth century to avoid being forcibly converted to Islam. The underdogs of Afghanistan are the Hazara. This Mongoloid, Shi'a people live mainly in the mountainous central region around Bamiyan, and in Kabul.

Years of war have disrupted the independence of many communities and have almost destroyed the fully nomadic way of life. Given the complexities of modern Afghanistan, it is hard to generalize about embroidery trends. Whereas the work of the Hazara is very distinct, the Uzbek and Turkmen share embroidery styles with neighbouring countries. The Pashtun – given their fierce independence and geographical distribution – produce a wide range of localized work.

CLOTHING STYLES

Western dress is gaining ground in Afghanistan, especially in towns and particularly for men, but older styles endure in rural areas. Although a survey of remote villages and valleys is at present impossible, much traditional clothing may still be worn. The basis of contemporary male clothing is the *shalwar-kameez*: baggy trousers, tied at the waist, with a loose straight shirt. The erosion of regional distinctions is exemplified by the traditional man's shirt of Kandahar: made by both Pashtun and Tajik, it is now marketed everywhere. These shirts – currently the most common items of embroidered male clothing – have a V-shaped yoke of fine geometric patterning, usually white on white. Shawls, often with embroidered borders, are worn with the *shalwar-kameez*; so too are waistcoats. Many men, especially those in Western dress, are bareheaded; others use the embroidered white cap typical of Islam. Sometimes older men wear a beautifully draped turban that conceals a brightly embroidered cap. Many regional accessories – floral embroidered sandals, for example, or embroidered belts – have apparently been abandoned.

Embroidered clothing on children is rarer than it was, but for special occasions small boys often wear the same Kandahar shirts and goldwork waistcoats as the men. Most children (male and female) wear Western dress or the *shalwar-kameez*.

The spectacularly decorative dress of Afghan women is still worn in rural areas, though no longer in the towns. Styles are immensely varied. If any kind of generalization is possible, it is that there are two distinct cuts of dress. The first style, worn within the Pashtun group by the Kakarh mountain people and the Koochi nomads, features an embroidered bodice joined at the waist to an embroidered skirt; sleeves are long and heavily embroidered. The second style, favoured in Nuristan and among the Baluch of the south, is a wide unshaped shift: embroidered from waist to hem, it has decorative gussets and wide sleeves. Women also use a long shawl or a *burqa* (concealing cloak). Clothing accessories include embroidered bands to wind round the hem of trouser legs (*puttees*) and a wide variety of caps. Embroidered shoes and boots, once popular, are rarely seen today.

DOMESTIC EMBROIDERY

Afghan women embroider a range of functional and decorative articles for their families and for the home, whether house or yurt. Cloths (termed *suzanis*) include wall hangings, curtains, bedcoverings, food covers and prayer mats. By extension, the saddle covers of bicycles may also be embellished with embroidery. In such a belligerent society as Afghanistan, it is not surprising that guns are highly prized. Pistol holsters are densely embroidered, as are covers for Lee Enfields and Kalashnikovs.

Embroideries made as dowry textiles by the Lakai Uzbek are true works of art. A sub-group of the Uzbek, the Lakai are horse-breeders; they came to Afghanistan in the 1930s to escape the Soviets and settled around the northern town of Kunduz. Their shamanistic designs, worked on decorative panels and wall-hangings, have a strange, forbidding power. The floral *suzanis* of the Uzbek are also made in northern Afghanistan, albeit with brighter and more naive depictions of flowers. Purses, pockets, tobacco pouches, containers for mirrors and watches, tiny bags to hold kohl and wrappers for the Koran are finely embroidered by all ethnic groups. The Hazara also embroider square prayer cloths (*mohr posh*) with religious motifs: mosques, minarets and the severed arms of Hazrat Abbas, martyr of the holy Shi'a site of Kerbela in Iraq.

Brass container for kohl, with decorative cover. Cotton and embroidery, with tassels of wool, shells and cowries. From the Baluch people of the Ghazni region. 70 x 39 cm (27^1/$_2$ x 15^1/$_2$ in).

PATTERNS AND PROTECTION

Most patterns are symbolic. The most prevalent motifs throughout the Central Asian region are those that are horned or hooked. Even straightforward geometric shapes – diamonds, triangles – have their edges serrated or ornamented with curling tendrils. Other motifs symbolizing the sun and stars hark back to the ancient cults of sun-and-fire worship, while those of the 'tree of life' and the pomegranate represent fertility. While the symbolism of many motifs is clear, that of others is not. Patterns are often distorted and their origins forgotten. The women who embroider do not know the meaning of many of the motifs they choose.

Amuletic embroidery (that which has a protective purpose) plays a significant role in Afghanistan in warding off the evil eye, disease and evil spirits in general. This defence can be in a splash of unexpected colour – as a vivid underarm gusset, for example. Amuletic motifs include horns, solar motifs, and a triangle with three pendants. Most Pashtun and some Hazara use tasselled and beaded edgings, the Pashtun being mainly of blue beads, a sure protection against the blue evil eye. For the Turkmen their narrow black-and-white cording is deemed to confront the power of the snake.

Beaded discs (*gul-i-peron*) are placed on the bodice, shoulders, or at the waist of Pashtun dresses, and also on animal trappings and bags of all kinds. Their amuletic power lies in the beads, shells, metal discs, gold thread and buttons that are incorporated into them. Pompoms and tassels are used by all groups. Triangles, as immensely powerful amulets, are embroidered with horns, floral motifs, stylized goddess figures or geometric designs and hung with tassels. Triangles are hung over doorways to protect the house and family, around the necks of domestic animals, or over the rear-view mirrors of vehicles. Headcovers worn by horses and camels are embroidered with solar motifs and hung with old

cotton reels, bells and tin lids: these rattle together and frighten evil spirits away.

Silk clothing was commonly worn every day, although dresses were often a mixture of fabrics. There is a certain purple silk fabric that helps to identify an embroidery as Afghan. Indigenous silk is still produced around Herat: this includes purple, but also red, green and black. Because of its high cost, silk is being replaced by synthetics or by cotton – home-grown or, more often, imported. Sheep and goats of the mountainous regions provide the wool for coats and the felt for floor coverings and tent pole bags (*okbash*). Many Afghan garments and embroidered objects have decorative printed cotton linings.

Typical of the embroidery of Afghanistan is the frequent use of one dominant stitch on each piece; that stitch will depend on the ethnic group of the embroiderer. (For the Pashtun it will also depend on their geographical location.) The work of the Lakai, for example, will either be in slanting blanket stitch, outlined in chain, or it will be in cross stitch – the two techniques will not be combined in the same piece. In Uzbek work, Bukhara couching is the defining stitch: laid threads are held by small stitches of the same thread, staggered to form a diagonal pattern. The traditional satin-stitch work of the Pashtun and Tajik of Kandahar is extremely fine. Metal threadwork features on many embroideries.

Most Afghan women have a predilection for bright colours – shocking pink, acid green, daffodil yellow – so that acrylic dyes were welcomed. The older natural dyes came from the same sources as in most parts of the world: red from madder or cochineal, yellow from saffron, turmeric or larkspur, orange from onion skins or walnut shells, blue from indigo, black from gall nut. Lemons give yellow, and both the leaves and fruit of mulberries provide mauve. Today several projects have revived the use of natural dyes.

PAST AND FUTURE

War and deprivation have inevitably brought profound changes to Afghanistan. Embroidery was once an essential part of life, whether urban or rural. A girl would be taught to embroider from the age of seven, as if her entire childhood were a preparation for the embroidering of her trousseau. During the last years before marriage, helped by friends and relatives, she would make new clothes for them to wear to the wedding, gifts for guests, clothes and presents for the bridegroom and his family, and textiles for her future home. She would even embroider a bag for the mirror in which she would see her bridegroom's face for the first time. This work was testimony to her skill and suitability for marriage.

Today bedcovers, pillowcases and other household textiles are still embroidered, but garments are often bought. In Kabul women purchase Western-style clothing for their husbands; the Kandahari shirt is now the only embroidered garment commonly seen on men and boys.

Financial constraints force women to spend more time making work to sell, and less time embroidering for the home and family. Rugs and jewellery, more profitable than embroideries, dominate the market. With the growing importance of commercial considerations, the role of aid organizations (both foreign and Afghan) has been crucial. DACAAR (Danish Committee for Aid to Afghan Refugees) was one of the first to use embroidery as a self-help tool for women. ECW (Educational Training Center for Poor Women and Girls of Afghanistan) was founded in Kabul in 1997 and aims to teach women embroidery and tailoring 'inside their houses hidden and secret from Taliban officials and Taliban government'. Some individual designers have set up shop in Kabul with moral support from the Afghan Business Women's Association. Organizations and designers help local women by providing materials and by buying finished embroideries. They also undertake to sell them – a challenging task in a land with few tourists.

Of course the fragile future of embroidery depends not only on official groups, but also on the women themselves. Once embroidery is divorced from its context – and the lifestyle that supported it is vanishing – an entirely new outlook is needed. That usually comes from harnessing old traditions and expertise into articles that have some relevance to modern life. Afghanistan is not alone in losing out to the modern world, but the resilience of its women, and their desperation to survive, gives some hope. The young mother embroidering in the mayhem of the bombing of Kandahar airport is a symbol, and still a hope for the future.

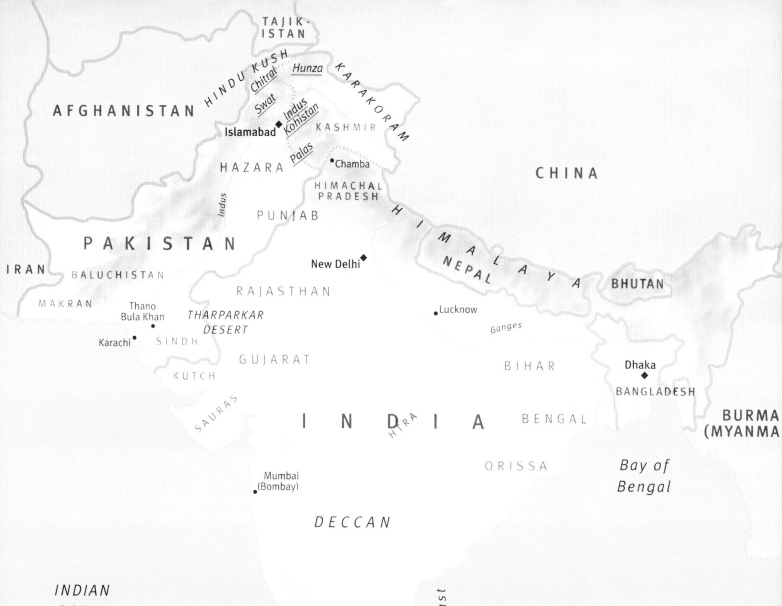

TAJIK-
ISTAN

HINDU KUSH
Chitral
Hunza
KARAKORAM

AFGHANISTAN

Swat

Indus
Islamabad   *Kohistan*
KASHMIR

Palas

HAZARA
• Chamba

HIMACHAL
PRADESH

CHINA

Indus

PUNJAB

H
I
M
A
L
A
Y
A

PAKISTAN

IRAN

New Delhi ◆

NEPAL

BHUTAN

BALUCHISTAN

RAJASTHAN

MAKRAN

Thano
Bula Khan •

*THARPARKAR
DESERT*

• Lucknow

Ganges

Karachi •

SINDH

GUJARAT

BIHAR

Dhaka ◆

BANGLADESH

KUTCH

I N D I A

BENGAL

BURMA
(MYANMA

*S
A
U
R
A
S*

H
T
R
A

ORISSA

*Bay of
Bengal*

Mumbai
(Bombay)
•

DECCAN

*INDIAN
OCEAN*

Coromandel Coast

SRI LANKA

◆ national capital

• city / town

EMBROIDERY FROM INDIA AND PAKISTAN

Brilliance of colour in an arid setting is the very essence of India and Pakistan. Embroidery, specific to each village and each tribe, adds to this intensity of colour. More significantly, it identifies and protects. The political boundary between India and Pakistan is largely irrelevant. The Rabari, for example, wandered across the Tharparkar desert: because they now live on both sides of the border, in Kutch and Sindh, their embroidery is Rabari – not Indian or Pakistani.

It is this region straddling the political frontier that is the hub of domestic embroidery in the Indian subcontinent. It comprises on the Indian side western Rajasthan, Gujarat, Saurashtra and Kutch, and on the Pakistani side Sindh. Punjab, to the north of this area and also now divided by the border, is another source of embroidery, as, in Pakistan, are the regions of Baluchistan and Hazara, and the high valleys of the North-West Frontier Province: Chitral, Swat and Indus. These are relatively isolated areas. Some – like eastern Sindh and the valleys of Indus Kohistan – are accessible only with a police permit, and often an armed guard. In India there is also the *kantha* quilt tradition of Bihar and Bengal in the east, and across the Deccan plateau the work of the Banjara.

Most of the embroidered textiles for which India was historically famous – such as the shawls of Kashmir and the floral work of Gujarat – were professionally made for the open market. Here, however, we are focusing on domestic embroidery made by women.

The 'hub' region is populated by herders, nomads and subsistence farmers. Their womenfolk, often living in dire poverty, are responsible for some of the richest embroidery in the world. Hindus and Muslims have intermingled over time, adopting many of each other's customs. There is one significant difference, however: Hindu women have greater freedom of movement than many Muslim women, who never leave their villages. Nomadic women, on the other hand, travel great distances, and are open to influences from the villages they pass through.

Despite their heavy workload, women regard embroidery as a social necessity. Taught by female relatives, many women start working on their dowry textiles at the age of six. Although embroidery is a lifelong pursuit, age and status determine how much time can be devoted to a given task. A doctor's wife from Makran in southern Baluchistan, for example, with servants to care for her children, may take an entire year to embroider a traditional dress for herself. The dowry of a Kanbi woman of Kutch usually takes five or six years to embroider.

CLOTHING AND DOMESTIC TEXTILES

In areas inhabited by several tribes and castes, clothing indicates the wearer's group and social status. Clothing worn by married women is more subdued in colour and pattern than that of young girls. Different groups have different garment styles. In Pakistan Muslim women wear a straight or flared shift with embroidery over the front bodice, shoulders and sleeves. Known by different names, this dress is used with loose trousers (*shalwar*) embroidered at the cuff. The costume of north-west India – Kutch, Rajasthan and Gujarat, and also Sindh – is an open-backed embroidered blouse (*chola*) and a gathered skirt (*gaghra*), generally embroidered at the hem with scattered motifs over the ground. Jath women of Kutch wear an ankle-length, full-skirted dress (*chori*), richly embroidered over the bodice front. The Banjara of the southern Deccan wear skirts with deep embroidered waistbands. An essential element in all these different costumes is the shawl, usually made of brightly printed, commercially produced fabric. (The sari does not form part of tribal dress. Those that are embroidered are professionally worked.)

Children's clothing imitates adult wear: the decoration on jackets, dresses and caps usually plays a talismanic role. Sling cradles – made for the home but used to carry babies when families are on the move – are also embroidered. For their menfolk, some tribal women embroider marriage shawls and scarves; others make elaborate guncovers and tobacco pouches. Decorated food covers, bags for many purposes, quilts and cushions are required for everyday domestic use. Door hangings are made to mark marriages, religious festivals and fairs.

FABRICS AND TECHNIQUES

Cotton fabric from India (hand-woven or factory-made) is generally used for clothing and domestic items. Some communities, however, prefer silk for festive and everyday wear. This is still true of the merchant classes of Kutch, although in Baluchistan vivid Chinese silks have been largely replaced by Japanese polyester. For shepherding groups like the Rabari, wool is the obvious choice. In Chitral, on Pakistan's north-western border with Afghanistan, men's dense natural woollen coats are embroidered with patterns of rams' horns.

Some fabrics are decorated by the tie-and-dye technique, whereby cloth is pinched into small balls and tightly tied with thread. Women's shawls are often tie-dyed by women and girls at home. A red background with white and yellow dots is the most common combination. The block printing of cotton cloth with a resist substance is done by Muslims and Hindus of the Khatri caste; embroidery adorns the block-printed marriage shawls of men of the Meghwal caste.

Certain villages are renowned for their expertise in dyeing. Chemical dyes have largely replaced the natural dyes for which India was once famous, but the unique vibrancy of the colour palette remains. Red is a significant and powerful colour throughout much of the world. Here its association with life and death, with fire and the power of the sun, with blood and vitality, imbue it with a potency that is considered auspicious for marriage and for the young: a girl's dress will be red, a widow's white.

Embroidery threads, manufactured in India or Pakistan, are sold by market stallholders and pedlars who understand regional colour

Opposite: Detail from a marriage canopy depicting a Hindu deity and a horse denoting prosperity. From Saurashtra, north-west India. See pp. 176–7.

preferences. Cotton and silk are being gradually overtaken by acrylics, to the detriment of workmanship. Some groups add sparkle by incorporating gold and silver – either jap threads or lurex – and small pieces of mirror glass, known as *shisha* or *alba*. These flashing additions sometimes play a talismanic role; so, too, do cowrie shells, red seeds, old zips, white buttons, silver trinkets, sequins, dangling triangular amulets, tassels and pompoms. They are thought to afford protection from the evil eye and from malevolent spirits that cause illness and death. With Baluchi dresses, decorative stitching and applied triangles serve a similar purpose: they surround the bodice slits that facilitate breast-feeding and 'protect' the mother's breasts.

All embroidery is based on either counting threads or following freely drawn lines. In the Indian subcontinent both techniques are used, although they rarely coincide in the same textile. Counted threadwork, known as *soof*, results in small geometric patterns. Drawn patterns are usually the work of the embroiderer herself. Stitches, often exquisitely executed, include chain, open chain, satin, surface darning, darning, stem, couching, herringbone and Cretan. These are found worldwide, but others – like the stitches that secure mirror glass – are unique to the Indian subcontinent. Quilting and appliqué, combined with other stitchery, are important techniques in many parts of India and Pakistan.

Almost all patterns are symbolic: motifs are thought to bring fertility, prosperity or protection from evil spirits. Hindu beliefs shape the designs on temple hangings, canopies and cloths. Lakshimi, goddess of wealth, is depicted as herself and also in the form of a lotus. Ganesh, the elephant god who ensures happiness, is a central motif on festive occasions. Animals, birds and insects have overtones of symbolism. Flowers, leaves and mango trees are depicted realistically, or often, in the case of flowers, as rosettes that merge into solar symbols. Mystical associations attach even to the motifs inspired by domestic life. Figurative styles are not to be found in Muslim work, which relies on geometric and linear designs. The elegant and disciplined embroideries of Muslims and Sikhs are characterized by their austerity of pattern, juxtaposition of colour and perfection of technique.

Through the ethnographically complex region of north-west India, in spite of enormous diversity and some mutual influence, certain distinguishing characteristics of colour, stitch, pattern and material can be determined in the work of the major tribes. Distinctive textiles are created by Hindu castes such as the Rabari, the Rajput and the Kanbi, as well as by Muslim groups like the Memon and the Jath. Textile traditions survive from generation to generation in India and Pakistan, so the decade of manufacture matters less than the tribe and place of origin.

The Punjab, lying in both India and Pakistan, is famous for embroidered cotton shawls known as *phulkaris*: whereas the patterns of Muslims and Sikhs are geometrical, those of the Hindus show lively scenes inspired by domestic life. In Pakistan the embroidered dresses of Baluchistan are distinguished by long tapering sleeves and a bright, contrasting underarm gusset. The hallmark of the central valley of Swat is a love of shocking pink. In the region of Hazara white cotton is patterned in a range of shades – from mauve to pink to red. There is an affinity in Hazara work with the *phulkaris* of Punjab.

In India, the work of the Banjara is pre-eminent. The Banjara were great traders: they criss-crossed the subcontinent before settling in the Deccan plateau in the nineteenth century. Today there is a northern and a southern style of embroidery, with minor variations. Many Banjara embroideries are edged with cowrie shells. The southern Banjara stitch wide waistbands for skirts, while all make bags and small cloths for various purposes. For marriages they embroider special bags for the bridegroom, as well as animal regalia such as bullock horn covers. North-eastern India and Bangladesh (which now lies outside India) is where *kantha* quilts and coverings are made. White cloth (originally from worn-out clothing) is stitched with symbolic Hindu motifs and other designs. In the past *kanthas* were embroidered by women for their families during the long rainy days of the monsoon. Now they are a marketed commodity – a success story in the current climate of change that is causing the erosion of folk art traditions.

TRADITION AND CHANGE

Several factors, including the education of girls, underlie the decline of embroidery in India and Pakistan. In the past a girl would devote much of her youth to the preparation of her dowry. Without the embroidered garments, domestic textiles, animal and marriage accoutrements and gifts for the bridegroom that had ritual significance in her social environment, a girl could not hope to find a husband. Today a girl with a university degree can manage without both the embroideries and the husband. And even if she merely finishes primary school, her early years will have been spent with pen and paper instead of thread and cotton. In India, at the same time, the caste system is gradually breaking down, threatening the age-old tradition of families. Exposure to the media is another significant factor: as television reaches rural homes, different lifestyles and ways of dressing are seen. Improved transportation and new roads bring commercially made products to previously isolated villages, where people lived by the work of their hands. Enforced migration – the result of political events – has led many people to settle in cities.

Not everything is negative, of course. In India there is encouragement and official support for handloom weaving and needlework. The embroidered textiles sold to tourists are less elaborate than traditional work, yet they keep alive a knowledge of stitches and techniques.

Much of the beauty of India comes from poverty: even rags can have a magical function. As India moves forward into a modern economy, its inspired tradition of folk embroidery is under threat, while that of Pakistan, its rural women still veiled and confined, may last a little longer.

CHINA

Chang Jiang (Yangtze)

SICHUAN

SICHUAN

ZUNYI

Fanjing
▲ *2493 m*

• Tongren

• Zunyi

TONGREN

BIJIE

HUNA

• Bijie

GUIZHOU

Jiuchaiping
▲ *2900 m*

• Weining

• Shidong

• Huangping

• Taijiang

• Jianhe

• Zhijin

• Guiyang

• Kaili

• Llupanshui

Leigong
▲ *2178 m*

• Nankai

• Huaxi

• Leishan

• Shuicheng

• Duyun

QIANDONGNAN

• Liuzhi

• Anshun

• Danzhai

YUNNAN

• Huishui

• Sandu

• Rongjiang

ANSHUN

QIANNAN

• Panxian

• Xingren

• Luodian

XINGYI

• Xingyi

GUANGXI

• Longlin

◆ province capital

• town

▲ mountain peak

MIAO TEXTILES FROM CHINA

The textiles featured here are those of the Miao people of Guizhou province, which lies in the subtropical zone of south-west China. The Miao are thought to have lived originally in the Huang He (Yellow River) basin, some 5,000 years ago. According to legend, they were beaten in battle by the Yellow Emperor and driven south to the middle reaches of the Chang Jiang (Yangtze River). By the Qin-Han Period (221 BC–AD 220), they had migrated to western Hunan and south-east Guizhou, and later to south Sichuan. But pressures from established indigenous groups and rival Han settlers – also from imperial troops pushing from the north – drove the Miao to constantly seek new territories. In 1413 Guizhou became an administrative province under the Ming Dynasty: imperial rule was ensured by the military invasion of tribal areas and by the subjugation of minorities. The Miao, who had settled in central and southern Guizhou and eastern Yunnan, were thus forced to continue migrating – into Thailand, Laos and Vietnam.

In south-west China, according to the 1992 census, there were seven million Miao – approximately four million of them living in Guizhou province. Today the Miao live peaceably with their neighbours, but in the nineteenth century they staged several bloody uprisings against the Han. The Miao and other tribal peoples resented the influx of Han settlers, and objected to high rents and taxes. During this period of unrest, some five million people died. Abject poverty persisted, especially among the Miao: observers during the first half of the twentieth century saw the Miao wearing rags and their children sharing clothes. Even today, many Miao remain below the poverty line.

The Miao can be divided into four main dialect groups and many subgroups. The only language in which they can all communicate is Putonghua (standard Mandarin). There is a strong oral tradition, but no written Miao language. One Miao subgroup has its own distinctive culture and dialect: the Gejia ('Ge family'), who live in and around Kaili, have for many years been seeking reclassification as a separate minority – as yet without success.

Because the Miao were one of the later groups to arrive in Guizhou, they settled chiefly in the mountains and rarely in the river valleys, which were already occupied by other minorities. Living as farmers, their most valued possession was their richly woven and embroidered festival costume. Today clothing remains the chief visual art form of the Miao. It identifies individuals as belonging to a specific group; it is also an indicator of family wealth. (The daughters of poor parents are kept busy in the fields, with little time to work on their costumes.) Crafts such as decorative wood carving and pottery are not practised, but specialized craftsmen – especially in the south-east – make superb silver crowns, necklaces, bracelets and plaques which are stitched on to girls' jackets.

The cultural role played by clothing has led the Han and some foreign anthropologists to identify Miao groups by their mode of dress.

(There are perhaps eighty different Miao costumes in Guizhou.) Nicknames, given by local people to particular groups, reflect aspects of their dress, such as 'Long and Short-Skirted Miao', 'White and Blue Miao', 'Flowery Miao' and so on. The Miao dislike these terms and identify themselves by their own dialect names.

STYLES, TECHNIQUES AND MOTIFS

Women's costumes are inventive variations on a basic theme: a long-sleeved jacket worn over a voluminous pleated skirt. On important occasions, several skirts or jackets may be worn together. Many groups have aprons (often worn front and back) and *puttees* or gaiters that cover the lower leg. Garments, assembled from narrow panels of hand-loomed cloth, are rarely shaped by cutting or tailoring. Jackets and skirts are decorated with woven strips and with wax-resist or embroidery pieces. Each group has its own distinctive hairstyle. The baby-carrier, a prestigious accoutrement and part of the dowry, is elaborately decorated using the finest techniques. Men's clothing once had decorative features similar to those of the women of their group, but much of this has now been lost.

Skirts are a key feature of Miao dress: finely pleated and often full, they are constructed and finished in various ways. One version uses between eight and fifty vertical panels of loom-width cloth: these are joined at the selvedges and pleated on to a waistband. Sometimes skirts of hemp or ramie have stitching across the waist-area: makers can tighten these stitches to produce a gathered effect similar to smocking. In many villages, tubular skirts are preferred: made from cotton, hemp or ramie, these ankle-length garments have no waistband – pleated daily by the wearer, they are held in place by a strong tie.

Both skirts and jackets may be embroidered. Women work on each small section individually. Colours are usually bright and vibrant, although older women in the south-east sometimes overdye finished garments with indigo. Embroidery patterns, drawn on to paper by older women, are sold at the market. Motifs in the south-east are chiefly zoomorphic, anthropomorphic and phyllomorphic; in other areas they tend to be geometric. Rich symbolism is found in most Miao embroidery – telling the story of the Miao migration, representing their creation myths and their heroes, and echoing their animistic beliefs.

Young Miao girls are taught by their mothers and grandmothers to spin, weave, dye and embroider. Every girl needs to wear her group's traditional costume for festivals and for marriage. If she has not acquired the necessary skills, her mother makes the costume for her.

Miao festivals take place in the low agricultural season. Jointly organized by villages of the same costume type, they often last for several days. Families flock to these events, carrying bundles of clothing on shoulder poles. In remote areas, people camp out on the hillside: they heat pre-cooked rice and pork on small fires, drink local alcohol, and talk long into the night. Young unmarried girls, who try to have a new costume for each festival, perform simple, slow-moving circle dances to the music of the lusheng pipes. This is their chance to be seen, in all their finery, by unmarried boys. Different groups have different courting rituals. It is said that unmarried Miao girls are judged by their future husbands on the quality of their clothing.

FIBRES AND WEAVING

Various textile fibres are used by the Miao of Guizhou. Hemp and ramie were once the chief source of yarn. These fibres, extracted from plant-stalks and laboriously prepared, are still used in the poorer west and drier central areas; elsewhere they are combined with cotton or synthetics. In the south of Guizhou where cotton is grown, the Miao prepare their own cotton textiles by ginning, spinning and weaving. In the wealthier south-east, which is too damp for cotton growing, cotton yarn and manufactured woven cotton cloth are bought at the markets. The north-west lies some 2,500 metres (8,200 ft) above sea level: here women wear woollen capes and gaiters made by itinerant felters; wool is also woven into the shoulders of hemp or ramie jackets for warmth. Silk has traditionally been used by wealthy families in the south-east – especially in the Kaili and Huangping areas where it is possible to raise silkworms. Local people used to process and dye silk thread; even today, some Miao women sell eggs and worms at the markets. Increasingly, however, silk thread is brought in from Shanghai.

There is a rich weaving tradition in Guizhou,

Miao girls from Jianhe county wearing festive costumes and elaborate silver jewellery.

especially in the south-east. The oldest weaving device is the body-tensioned backstrap loom; treadle-operated frame looms with four shafts are also used. Cloth for skirts, jackets and trousers is usually tabby- or plain-woven. Lozenge twill weaves – and, more rarely, an alternating float weave – are found in the south-east. Although cloth is normally dyed after weaving, a few groups use dyed yarns to create stripes and checks. Supplementary weft techniques are common in fabrics woven from wool, silk and cotton. Patterns for the decorative areas of garments and for baby-carriers are sometimes extremely complex, featuring birds, butterflies and geometrical designs put in by hand. The back-panels and decorative sleeve pieces of jackets often incorporate weft-faced ribbon-like strips: woven in groups on large frame looms, they are cut out and sewn down.

Several groups weave warp-striped coloured silk ribbons as decorative bands to be sewn on to skirts. Gaiters, *puttees* and aprons are frequently tied with narrow warp-faced cotton and silk bands woven on small frame looms. Similar, slightly wider bands are used as ties on baby-carriers. Gejia women use the backstrap loom to make waist and *puttee* ties: they sit on the ground and tension the warp on their big toes. Backstrap weavers from other Miao groups prefer to sit on a chair: they tension the cloth beam around their body and attach the far-end of the warp to a post.

DYES

Indigo is the most popular dye in Guizhou. Indigo paste is prepared from the leaves of either *Polygonum tinctorium* or – more usually – *Strobilanthes cusia*. Domestic dyeing is commonly done by women, who reconstitute the indigo paste with ash and water in a wooden dye vat. For up to twenty-four days, hand-woven and bought fabrics are repeatedly dipped and aired until they turn dark-blue. There are many dyeing taboos: if a pregnant woman goes near the vat, the vat must be restarted.

Shiny indigo-dyed cloth is prized by the Miao. Calendering is done by folding the material and beating it with a wooden mallet on a flat stone. Male professional dyers, and some families, use a huge 'rocking stone'. With this technique, which is shared with the Han Chinese, the cloth is put

on a roller which is placed under the stone. The man then stands on the stone, rocking from side to side and supporting himself on the rafters.

Chemical dyes have been available in China since 1870, and today the dye vat is often spiced with a chemical that intensifies the blue colour and shortens the dyeing process. Although home dyeing remains common, many women now take their cloth and yarn to be chemically dyed by professional male dyers. In Huangping Miao dyers use an aniline colourant (which normally

Miao girls wearing festive dress and silver jewellery in Rongjiang county.

dyes purple) to give a glistening green-bronze tinge to cotton and silk cloth. Other villagers dislike sitting next to these Miao on a bus, because the dye – not being fast – can rub a purple colour on to their clothes.

When a non-absorbent substance or 'resist' is applied to fabric, it protects selected areas from dyes such as indigo. Skirts, jackets and turbans of hemp and cotton are patterned by the wax resist method. Although beeswax has traditionally been used, paraffin wax is also popular; in Huishui tree resin (*Liquidambar formosana*) is preferred. Bamboo sections, or the quills of chickens and even porcupines, can serve as waxing tools, but most practitioners apply heated wax using specially made metal tools with bamboo handles. (A skilled waxer may work with twenty such tools of different sizes.) The Gejia excel at wax resist: their designs include geometric patterns and bold floral motifs on a blue ground. Some villagers in central Guizhou paint yellow, green and red natural or chemical dyes on their finished designs using hemp sticks or brushes. Other communities achieve repeat designs on skirts with stencils. In the north-west stitch resist techniques offer an alternative to wax resist.

TRADITION AND CHANGE

In China, as in other parts of the world, the pressure for change is affecting traditional textiles. Although most Miao women wear traditional clothing on market days and special occasions, it is often combined with factory-made items for everyday use. Miao men commonly wear 'Mao' suits or Western-style garments – only a few own distinctive clothing for festivals. Miao girls, influenced by television programmes, are increasingly adopting 'modern' dress; some attend school and later find jobs in distant towns, where they are exposed to global fashion trends.

After the establishment of the People's Republic of China in 1949, song and dance teams were formed to promote socialist values while emphasizing cultural identity. The best troupes appear on television and promote China abroad. Over time the traditional clothing of Miao performers has mutated into a stage costume: skirts are shortened; indigo-dyed garments are embroidered with beads and sequins. Because performers are admired, these changes influence clothing in general. Tourism is another factor. Westerners have been visiting Guizhou since the end of the 1980s, when the Government first 'opened' selected villages to foreigners. Local song and dance troupes, wearing 'exotic' versions of their traditional clothing, entertain visitors from other parts of China and overseas. Much-needed revenue is generated by the sale of souvenirs and hastily-made textiles, many of inferior quality. The demand for fine costumes is often met by dealers, who scour villages and buy up traditional work. One remote village is said to have given a Miao dealer ten festival costumes in exchange for a pig for a feast. With the rise of entrepreneurial socialism in China, the Miao are focusing less on their own identity. The pressures of modernization will no doubt continue to have a major impact on the traditions and textile cultures of Guizhou.

TEXTILES FROM GUATEMALA

Guatemala, the northernmost republic of Central America, lies between the Caribbean Sea and the Pacific Ocean. Bordered by Mexico, Belize, Honduras and El Salvador, it embraces snow-clad mountains and volcanoes, fertile coastal plains and dense rain forests. These were the territories of the ancient Maya, whose civilization reached its height in AD 300–900. Conquered by Spanish forces in the sixteenth century, the Maya have ceaselessly asserted their right to maintain their own way of life. Today several million Maya still speak numerous languages and preserve their distinctive culture. Throughout the south-west highlands women continue to weave and wear traditional clothing. Each Maya community has its own dress style: garments and designs assert an ethnic identity that is deeply rooted in history.

Women learn the art of weaving from mothers and grandmothers. The *huipil*, which resembles a rectangular blouse, is the most important item of a woman's *traje* (costume). Long or short, it is made from one, two or three panels stitched together; sides are left open, or sewn as far as the armhole. A carefully woven *huipil* with a complicated design could take several weeks to complete. The *tzute* (all-purpose carrying cloth) is also home-woven. In some places, women still weave other parts of their *traje*: the skirt, sash and hair-ribbon. More usually, however, these are made by specialist weavers using various types of loom. Skirt lengths, cut to size, are sold in most local markets. Maya women favour two styles of skirt. The commonest type, about 3 m (9 ft 10 in) long, is wrapped around the waist or made into a tube. The second type, consisting of 6–9 m (20–30 ft) of material, is gathered on a drawstring. Although new garments are sometimes made for festivals and weddings, the components of a woman's *traje* do not change with the seasons. Clothing is only discarded when it is beyond further use. Even then the wearer may extend the life of a richly patterned section, cutting it out for inclusion in a future garment.

For political and practical reasons, Maya men rarely wear *traje* in their daily lives. In Sololá and villages near Lake Atitlán, however, traditional clothing has been retained. It also persists in the Cuchumatánes Mountains: in the village of Todos Santos, males of all ages wear red trousers striped with white, and white shirts striped in red. Shoulder bags, crocheted by the men of Todos Santos, remain important accessories – even in distant towns and villages where traditional male dress has been abandoned.

Special clothing is still worn in several communities by members of *cofradías* (religious brotherhoods attached to the church). Men in Chichicastenango retain distinctive jackets and trousers for processions and *costumbres* (local customs). Women connected with the church or married to a *cofradía* member may also use ceremonial clothing. In Quezaltenango, a voluminous white muslin garment is worn: shaped like a *huipil*, it serves as a veil with the neck opening framing the wearer's face; in Tecpán, the everyday *huipil* is covered by a larger *sobrehuipil*.

In addition to the weaving of textiles for

Weaver from the Cakchiquel Maya village of Patzún selling textiles on the pavement in Guatemala City.

personal use and local consumption, there is a growing trade in crafts designed for tourists and for export. Some travellers are happy to buy traditional items of clothing, but most prefer non-traditional mementos such as purses and cushion covers. The sale of these goods provides makers with much-needed income. Many weavers join cooperatives and manage their own resources.

FIBRES AND DYES

Cotton, the most widely used textile fibre in Guatemala, is grown on plantations in the Pacific lowlands. It is harvested by the highland Maya, who see this annual migration as an unpleasant but necessary way to augment their household income. Two types of cotton are indigenous to Central America: a long-staple white cotton (*Gossypium hirsutum*) and a short-staple brown cotton (*G. mexicanum*). Additional raw cotton is imported from Nicaragua and the USA. Ready-spun, ready-dyed cotton is also imported.

Sheep's wool, introduced after the conquest, is chiefly produced in the mountainous south-west. Hot springs in Momostenango aid the finishing processes and the felting of woollen goods such as blankets. Lengths of woollen suiting are woven not just in Momostenango but also in Chichicastenango, Nahualá and Sololá. Although acrylic is a man-made fibre, it can be spun to resemble a 'lofty' wool: the resulting yarn, less costly than wool and brilliantly coloured, is an increasingly popular option. Silkworms are not cultivated in Guatemala, so all silk is imported. Although expensive, it is prized for its lustre and its affinity for dyes. Silk floss (unspun silk) is often used to embellish special garments and items for church use. Rayon, an artificial silk, is also lustrous – and considerably cheaper.

Chemical dyes, invented in 1856, have replaced most natural colourants. Cochineal, a crimson dyestuff derived from the dried bodies of female insects, was much used by nineteenth-century dyers of wool and silk. Cochineal was later supplanted by alizarin – a synthetic red dye patented in 1871. Indigo, like cochineal, was once exported in vast quantities. Valued for its subtle blue tones, indigo has nevertheless been largely replaced – first by a synthetic version, then by cheaper alternatives.

The dyer's art finds its full expression with *jaspe* – the tie-dyeing of warp or weft threads before they are woven. *Jaspe* weft threads pattern many *tzutes*, forming intricate designs: these include names and greetings. Shawls incorporate *jaspe* warp threads that alternate with plain-coloured warp stripes. Dyers often use the roadway to stretch out long threads: family members – even tiny children – are kept busy binding predetermined sections. *Jaspe* designs have gently blurred edges, caused when the colour in the dye bath seeps beyond these bindings.

TECHNIQUES AND MOTIFS

To fully appreciate the beauty of Guatemalan textiles, it is useful to understand the labour-intensive nature of weaving techniques. Traditionally, cloth is woven by women on the backstrap loom (also known as the hip loom, body-tensioned loom or stick loom). To 'dress' or prepare this highly portable loom, weavers stretch warp threads between two parallel rods. The back rod is tied to a tree or post; a strap, attached to the front rod, encircles the weaver's hips and allows her to control the tension.

The backstrap loom is suited to the creation of small and medium-sized cloth panels. For blankets and other large textiles, the European four-shaft treadle loom is preferred. Introduced after the conquest and chiefly used by men, this heavy wooden structure permits different cloth constructions; it can also accommodate long warp threads measuring 65 m (213 ft) and more. Controlled by the weaver's feet, the warps rise and fall at speed. A small ribbon loom, perhaps unique to Guatemala, combines some aspects of the backstrap loom with those of the treadle loom. Two other, more sophisticated looms are associated with Quezaltenango and San Marcos. One is the draw loom; the other – a development of the draw loom – is the jacquard. Both make it possible to weave intricate repeating patterns the length of the fabric.

Tapestry, a freer form of weaving akin to picture making, is used for hair ribbons, particularly in the vicinity of Totonicapán. In Alta Verapaz, near Cobán, exquisite all-white cloth with inlay designs is created by skilled gauze-weavers. Embroidery, often confused with brocading by early travellers, is a popular way of embellishing finished cloth. Sometimes it has a practical function. Necklines are embroidered to prevent fraying; cloth panels may be joined by a colourful *randa* (band of stitching).

Stripes and checks pattern many garments, often providing a background for the brocaded designs that convey the ethnicity of the wearer. These designs are not drawn: they are carried in the weaver's head, because she has been familiar with them since early childhood. Some are abstract. Triangles, diamonds, lozenges, chevrons and zigzags lend themselves to the technique of weaving, and may have a symbolic role. However, many weavers are surprised to be asked about the 'meaning' of designs.

The flora and fauna of Guatemala inspire numerous motifs: lions, jaguars, opossums, dogs, monkeys, quetzals, peacocks, owls, bats, turkeys, hens and ducks. Many of these creatures were mentioned in the *Popol Vuh* – the great Maya creation epic. Other popular motifs include pine and ceiba trees, maize plants and human figures. Although the double-headed eagle was conferred on the Quiché by the Spanish Crown, it was already a familiar image within Maya culture. Today it appears on *huipiles* from Chuarrancho and textiles from Nahualá. Older *huipiles* from Chichicastenango displayed a highly stylized version on the central panel; these same *huipiles* embodied a visual reference to the four cardinal points – North, South, East and West.

ANCIENT AND MODERN

Some elements of Guatemalan costume are extremely ancient. Stone reliefs, figurines and paintings on walls and pots showed women dressed – much as they are today – in elegant *huipiles* and wrap-around skirts secured by waist-sashes. Of the many garments once worn by men, however, only capes, hipcloths and sandals persist today. After the Spanish conquest, most items of male clothing were replaced by European styles of dress. In some places, women's wrap-around skirts have similarly given way to gathered skirts on waistbands.

In recent times, indigenous traditions have again been under threat. Catholic beliefs and festivals, for so long the mainstay of Maya family life, are being undermined by the spread of Evangelical movements. Many missionaries discourage the use of traditional clothing (especially when it is linked with *cofradía* activities) and persuade women to abandon *traje*. Far more serious has been the legacy of civil war. Between 1960 and 1996 – a period when some 200,000 Guatemalans were killed or disappeared – indigenous people were savagely targeted by the state. The horrors of this period led many indigenous men to shun village-specific clothing while adopting cheap shirts and trousers imported from North America.

Increased interest in the Maya has stimulated tourism and the trade in crafts. Although many items are mass-produced, countless women continue to weave in traditional ways. Some interpret existing designs using non-traditional colours and yarns; others are reviving designs from the past with a new sense of pride. With better schooling and improved communications,

Cakchiquel Maya weaver holding up a two-web *tzute* (head covering) in
Santa María de Jesús, Sacatepéquez, Guatemala.

young women are taking an interest in the
indigenous garments of other towns; some are
happy to wear an alternative *huipil* to their own,
if it pleases them. They are following fashion, like
young people everywhere, embracing new ideas
and rejecting old ones. Since the 1930s, literature
on Guatemalan textiles has been predicting their
imminent decline. Some elements – like the
photogenic red headgear of Santiago Atitlán –
have fallen into disuse except among the very old.
But a new sense of cultural identity, coupled with
the cross-fertilization of ideas, would seem to
suggest that the prophets of doom are mistaken.

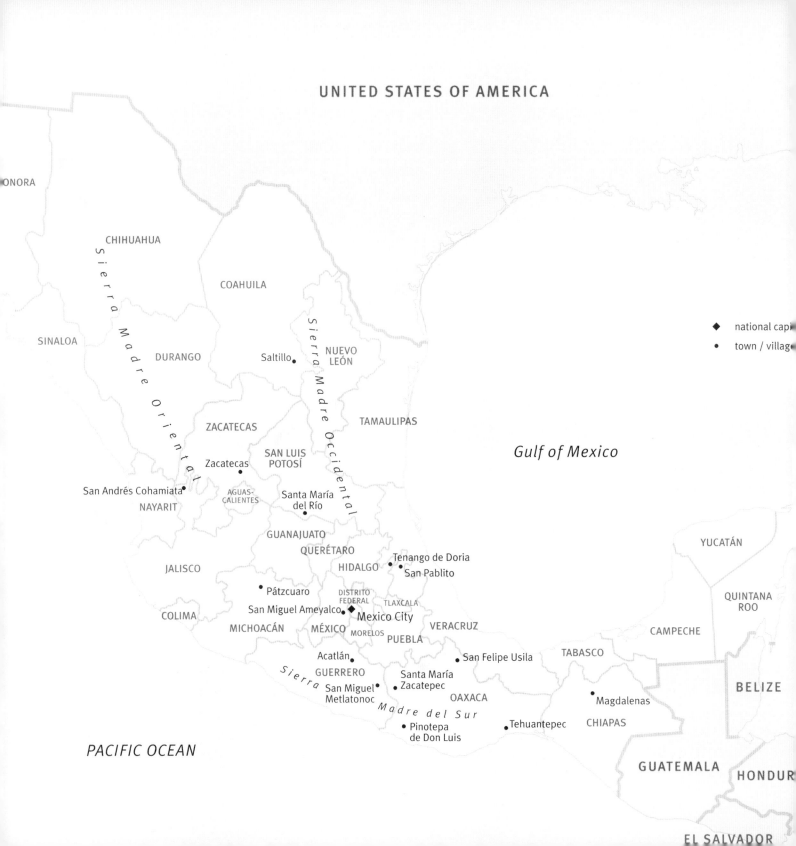

UNITED STATES OF AMERICA

SONORA

CHIHUAHUA

COAHUILA

Sierra Madre Oriental

SINALOA

DURANGO

Saltillo •

NUEVO
LEÓN

ZACATECAS

Sierra Madre Occidental

TAMAULIPAS

Zacatecas •

SAN LUIS
POTOSÍ

◆ national cap[ital]

• town / villag[e]

Gulf of Mexico

San Andrés Cohamiata •

AGUAS-
CALIENTES

Santa María
del Río •

NAYARIT

GUANAJUATO

YUCATÁN

QUERÉTARO

JALISCO

HIDALGO

Tenango de Doria
•
• San Pablito

QUINTANA
ROO

• Pátzcuaro

DISTRITO
FEDERAL

COLIMA

San Miguel Ameyalco •
◆ Mexico City

TLAXCALA

MICHOACÁN

MÉXICO

VERACRUZ

CAMPECHE

MORELOS

PUEBLA

Acatlán •

GUERRERO

Santa María
• Zacatepec

San Felipe Usila •

TABASCO

Sierra

San Miguel
Metlatonoc •

• Magdalenas

BELIZE

OAXACA

Madre del Sur

Tehuantepec •

CHIAPAS

• Pinotepa
de Don Luis

PACIFIC OCEAN

GUATEMALA

HONDUR[AS]

EL SALVADOR

TEXTILES FROM MEXICO

Few countries have such extreme variations of climate and vegetation as Mexico. Landscapes include arid deserts, fertile valleys, tropical forests, deep canyons and high mountain peaks. Mexico covers a vast area of almost 2 million square kilometres (760,000 square miles). Contrasting environmental conditions have influenced the evolution of clothing throughout Mexico's long history. Ancient stone carvings, murals, painted manuscripts and terracotta figures show a wide range of dress styles. Today distinctive clothing is worn in rural areas where indigenous cultures are strong. It is hard to establish reliable census figures in remote regions, but current estimates put Mexico's indigenous population – divided into sixty-two language groups – at around ten million.

The origins of the Maya go back more than 4,000 years. At their height (AD 300–900), they excelled as architects, sculptors and astronomers. Based on a loose federation of city states, Maya civilization stretched across the Yucatán Peninsula and Chiapas in Mexico; it also took in Belize, Guatemala and parts of Honduras. Like their ancestors, the modern Maya speak several languages. In the Chiapas highlands, for example, there are over 300,000 speakers of Tzotzil. To the west of the Maya zone, important cultures were forged after AD 300 by the Zapotec and the Mixtec. The present-day state of Oaxaca is home to their descendants and to other peoples such as the Chinantec. In central Mexico, the most widely spoken indigenous language is Nahuatl. This was the language of the Aztecs (or *Mexica*), who settled in the Valley of Mexico after AD 1200 and established a vast empire. Today nearly two million Nahua – as Nahuatl-speakers are termed – live chiefly in the states of Puebla, Veracruz, Hidalgo, Guerrero and San Luis Potosí.

CLOTHING

In most indigenous communities, textile skills centre on the creation of clothing. Ancient techniques such as spinning and weaving are passed down from generation to generation, but the European legacy should not be overlooked. After the Spanish conquest of 1521, settlers introduced new materials, techniques and clothing styles. This fusion, over nearly five centuries, has given rise to a wide range of garments and design motifs.

In regions where women's clothing has changed comparatively little, wrap-around skirts are worn. Some are rectangular, but others are seamed to form a tube. Each morning, when the wearer puts on her skirt, she arranges the cloth in a series of folds or pleats held in place by a waist-sash. Also of pre-conquest origin are the *huipil* and the *quechquemitl*. The *huipil* resembles a sleeveless, rectangular tunic made from one, two or three panels. The *quechquemitl* is best described as a closed shoulder-cape. European-style garments include skirts on waistbands, aprons and blouses. The *rebozo* (rectangular shawl) evolved during the colonial period to become a national symbol of womanhood.

Male indigenous dress has undergone more

changes than female dress. Men wore loincloths, hipcloths, sashes, tunics, capes and imposing headdresses before the conquest, but were subsequently persuaded to adopt shirts and trousers. In recent decades many indigenous men have been driven by economic necessity to seek work far from home and to abandon their own garments in favour of jeans and T-shirts. And yet, despite the pressure for change, some communities prefer traditional clothing styles. Shirts and trousers may be European in inspiration, but makers interpret them in various ways. In parts of Chiapas and Oaxaca, for example, garments are assembled from home-woven panels without recourse to zips, buttons or pockets. Even in areas where garments are made from factory-produced cloth, these may be embellished with embroidery.

The *sarape* is a rectangular blanket, often with an opening for the head. Like the *rebozo*, the sarape evolved under Spanish rule. After 1821, when Mexico became independent, foreign travellers likened the *sarape* to a 'national institution'. Wealthy men wore splendid examples: woven from silk, gold and silver metallic threads, they often displayed complex geometric designs. Contemporary *sarapes* are more affordable but less ornate.

Although most indigenous textiles are made to be worn, great care goes into the making of *servilletas* (all-purpose cloths) used to wrap or cover food. During religious festivals, these are displayed on altars in homes and churches. Non-traditional items such as tablecloths and wall-hangings generate much-needed revenue. Sometimes the tourist market inspires great creativity: decorative cloths embroidered by the Otomí of Tenango de Doria and San Pablito combine commerce with joyful exuberance and freedom of expression.

FABRICS AND DYES

White cotton is native to Mexico; so too is the rarer, toffee-brown strain known as *coyuche*. Preparation is long and arduous: as in ancient times, spinning is done with the aid of a spindle weighted with a clay whorl. Wool, introduced by Spanish settlers, is popular in mountainous regions. Silk plantations were successfully established after the conquest, then banned by royal decree. Small-scale production continues in parts of Oaxaca, where insects and mulberry trees survive, but most weavers and embroiderers rely on imported silk. In recent decades, shortages and spiralling costs have forced many women to abandon natural fibres in favour of synthetic ones: rayon serves as a cheap substitute for silk; acrylic is fast replacing wool.

Natural dyes, still used in some communities, include inorganic substances such as iron oxide. Flowers, fruits, lichens and other localized plant dyes play a vital role. Reddish tones may be obtained with brazilwood; indigo (*Indigofera suffruticosa*) gives several shades of blue. Two animal dyes, greatly valued before the conquest,

Lavishly embroidered clothing is worn to celebrate the Feast of the Assumption in Tehuantepec, Oaxaca state.

47

persist today. Cochineal (*Dactylopius coccus*) is a delicate insect which feeds on cacti. It provides colouring matter ideally suited to wool and silk: shades range from crimson to reddish-black. On the Pacific coast of Oaxaca, cotton is dyed purple with the secretion of molluscs (*Purpura patula*). While some dyes stain fibres directly, others are fixed by substances such as alum or urine. Indigo and purpura require oxidization.

Before the invention of chemical dyes, natural dyes were sometimes used in conjunction with *ikat*. With this technique, threads are patterned before they are woven: tightly bound at predetermined intervals, they are dipped in a dye bath. (Covered areas are described as 'reserved'.) Many eighteenth- and nineteenth-century *rebozos* were elegantly patterned by this method. Today costly examples of *ikat*-dyed silk (and cheaper rayon versions) are still woven in Santa María del Río in the state of San Luis Potosí.

WEAVING AND EMBROIDERY

Skilled weavers create cloth of great beauty and complexity. In indigenous communities many women continue to clothe their families using the native backstrap loom. Although the apparatus is simple, it is extremely versatile. Traditional garments are not tailored in the European manner: instead they are assembled directly from squares or rectangles of cloth. Texture and patterning are crucially important. Brocading, often mistaken for embroidery, uses supplementary weft threads to embellish garments with flowers, birds, animals and

Tzeltal Maya weaver wearing a ceremonial *huipil* in Magdalenas, Chiapas.

geometric motifs. Gauze-weaving is another ancient skill: warp threads, crossed by hand and secured by the weft, form open-meshed cloth with the delicacy of lace.

The treadle loom, introduced after the conquest, is faster than native looms. Cloth panels are longer and wider. Weavers, predominantly male, supply local people with shawls, skirt lengths and blankets or *sarapes*. When *sarapes* and rugs are tapestry-woven, discontinuous weft threads cover the warp threads to form patterns in the cloth. Eighteenth- and nineteenth-century tapestry weavers in centres like Saltillo, in the state of Coahuila, created dazzling effects: characteristic designs included small triangles, rhomboids, hour-glasses and ovals grouped round a central lozenge or medallion.

Embroidery has a long history in Mexico. Archaeological cloth fragments prove that decorative stitching was sometimes used on pre-conquest clothing. European needlework skills were taught in mission centres, while further inspiration was provided by textiles imported from China and the Philippines. Today Mexican women embroider home-woven and bought cloth using satin, running, stem and other stitches.

There are many other ways of embellishing garments. With drawn threadwork, individual threads are removed from finished cloth to create open-meshed areas of patterning. Factory-made ribbons may be sewn down to conceal seams and reinforce neck openings, or left hanging in colourful cascades. Where *rebozos* and waist-sashes have long warp ends, these are finger-knotted to provide decorative fringes. Love of ornamentation is further exemplified by the tassels and pompoms that adorn shoulder-bags.

TRADITION AND INNOVATION

Some of the motifs that characterize indigenous clothing are inherited from earlier times: these include stepped frets, zigzag lines, hooks and other geometric forms. Numerous designs, by contrast, evolved after contact with Europe, the Near East, China and the Philippines. Flowers and foliage adorn many textiles and share this mixed heritage, as do designs inspired by the animal world. Some designs are unequivocally European in their inspiration: horses, introduced into Mexico at the time of the conquest, now pattern many garments. Double-headed birds may be linked with the crowned Habsburg eagle of colonial times, or they may be a pre-conquest survival. Whereas some designs are naturalistic, others are highly stylized and often indecipherable to outsiders. For the Huichol – who live high in the Sierra Madre, where the states of Jalisco and Nayarit meet and who have largely rejected Christianity – textiles serve as visual prayers and link wearers with their deities. Zigzag lines that suggest lightning are associated with rain, while the deer is viewed as an incarnation of both maize and peyote (the hallucinatory cactus).

Indigenous clothing has never been static: it is this mixture of ancient and modern, tradition and innovation, that lends such vitality to Mexico's wide range of styles. For the Mexican tourist industry, 'quaint customs' and 'exotic costumes' are an obvious attraction. In real life, however, the Huichol and other groups face discrimination from local people who equate the wearing of traditional clothing with backwardness. It would be tragic if native dress, together with textile skills that have endured for centuries, should disappear altogether from Mexico. One sign of hope may lie with the cultural tenacity of indigenous leaders in Chiapas and elsewhere who see traditional clothing as an integral part of indigenous identity and a reason not for shame but pride.

COLOMBIA

Quito ◆

ECUADOR

Marañon

BRAZIL

A

Huaca Prieta ●

Guitarrero
Cave ●

Trujillo ●

N

La Galgada ●

Ucayali

PERU

Chancay ●

D

Machu Picchu
●

Lima ◆

Wari ●

Cuzco ●

Paracas Peninsula

E

Nazca ●

Lake
Titicaca

La Paz ◆

BOLIVIA

Tiwanaku ◆

S

Lake
Poopó

Arica ●

Isluga ●

PACIFIC
OCEAN

PARAGUAY

Tulan ●

CHILE

ARGENTINA

TEXTILES FROM THE ANDES

The ancient peoples of the Andes lived in a dramatically diverse realm dominated by the world's longest mountain range. The *cordillera* of the Andes, which runs from north to south for some 7,000 km (4,300 miles), incorporates precipitous mountain peaks, high plateaux and fertile valleys. The Amazon river basin stretches to the east; to the west lie the arid deserts of the Pacific coast. South-American societies successfully adapted to the extraordinary demands of these very different environments. What many hold in common is that they invested much of their creative energy in the making and embellishing of clothing and fine fabrics. Both lowland and highland cultures boast some of the most varied, textile-oriented traditions in world history although differing preservation means that some are more fully documented than others. The Inkas, centred on highland Peru, were but the last in a long sequence of Andean civilizations to be deprived of their power by Spanish forces after 1532.

THE MOST ANCIENT TEXTILES

In most regions of the world ceramics preceded textiles, but the opposite is true in South America: the earliest fired ceramics have been dated to around 1800 BC, while the oldest known examples of fibrework were probably made as long ago as 8500 BC. Found in the Guitarrero cave in the central highlands of Peru, these finger-manipulated fabric fragments were created by the pre-loom methods of twining, looping and

knotting. Twining was the technique used *c.* 2500 BC by the inhabitants of Huaca Prieta, a small fishing village on Peru's north coast, to make elaborately patterned textiles from domesticated cotton (*Gossipium barbadense*). Some designs were abstract, featuring diamonds and chevrons, but others included stylized representations of the natural world.

The heddle-operated loom, which evolved *c.* 1800 BC, was used to weave cloth at Chavín de Huántar in Peru's north-central highlands. Between 1000 and 200 BC this influential ceremonial centre developed a distinct art-style and made remarkable advances in textiles, metallurgy, architecture and ceramics. Large polychrome cotton cloths were painted with complex religious imagery. Examples in Chavín style have been found at Karwa, a distant burial site on Peru's south coast. Like many other surviving weavings of the pre-Hispanic era, these were preserved by the dry desert environment allowing burial practices and contexts to be better understood.

Some of the most outstanding pre-Hispanic textiles come from burial sites on the Paracas Peninsula. The cemeteries of the Paracas culture, which flourished from approximately 600 BC to AD 100, have preserved hundreds of mummy bundles: the bodies of the dead, accompanied by pottery vessels and other grave goods, were richly dressed and wrapped in layer upon layer of fine cloth. These textiles are remarkable for their vivid colour spectrum. The weavers of Paracas used camelid hair imported from the highlands as well

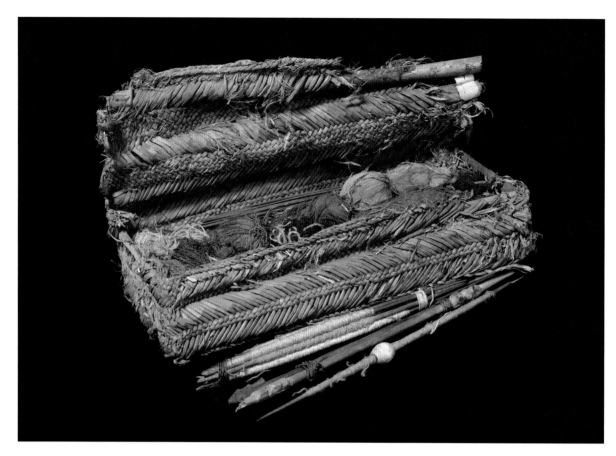

Pre-Hispanic rectangular plaited workbasket with hinged lid containing spindles and other items. Probably from the central coast of Peru. L. 24 cm (9 in). Given by Miss E. Tucker.

as coastal cotton. The camelids (alpacas and llamas) all provide 'wool' that readily accepts dyes.

The rise of embroidery at Paracas permitted a seemingly limitless range of interlocking design motifs. Intricately worked in stem stitch and backstitch, these included animals, birds, serpents and fish that sometimes combined several elements in a single figure. With human subjects such as dancers and warriors, the body and head were shown from the front, while the legs generally appeared in profile. Some of these splendidly costumed figures may represent humans impersonating gods and acting as intermediaries between the everyday and supernatural worlds.

Nasca culture (*c.* AD 100 to 750), which developed on a desert plain on the southern coast of Peru, was heavily influenced by the creative achievements and textile arts of Paracas. In both cultures cotton and camelid hair were spun with the aid of a spindle, and woven on a body-tensioned backstrap. Dozens of colour hues were achieved with a small number of dyestuffs from plant and animal sources. These included indigo (*Indigofera suffruticosa*), various species of madder (including *Relbunium ciliatum*), annatto (*Bixa orellana*), a yellow-brown colourant from native plants, cochineal (*Dactylopius coccus*) and a purple dye obtained from a snail-like mollusc (*Purpura patula pansa*). In addition to embroidery, weavers decorated finished textiles in a variety of ways. These included the addition of feathers, ornaments of worked shell, coloured stones and wafer-thin sheets of gold. Garments and ceremonial cloths were sometimes painted with complex designs, given fringes or ties, and edged with small three-dimensional figures. These were representations of people, animals and birds, needleworked in a cross-knit loop stitch that resembles knitting. Very occasionally an entire garment was created by this process. Braiding and sprang (a two-ended method of interlinking a set of lengthways threads) were also used to form Paracas and Nasca fabrics.

CREATIVE DEVELOPMENTS

These structural innovations were taken in new creative directions by such cultures as the Moche, Tiwanaku, Wari, Chimú, Chancay and ultimately the Inkas. Every known weaving technique was used in pre-Hispanic Peru. Twill, double and even treble weaves were common, as was weft-brocading. Some textiles were woven with a discontinuous warp and weft. With this method, unique to the Andean region, 'scaffold' threads (later removed) created a temporary grid: this enabled the weaver to interlock warp and weft threads so that neither extended across the entire cloth. Wari culture (*c.* AD 500 to 900) developed in the mountainous valley of Ayacucho in central Peru and had close links with Tiwanaku (*c.* AD 300–1100) in present-day Bolivia. Wari weavers created extraordinarily complex textiles using discontinuous warp and weft yarns of camelid hair; after the weaving was completed, cloth was sometimes tie-dyed different colours to create units of geometric patterning.

Tapestry weaving, which had begun to replace embroidery as the dominant technique in the late Nasca period, was another Wari specialty. Sumptuous weft-faced tunics (so-called because the cotton warp was altogether concealed by the discontinuous camelid-hair weft) were densely patterned with a profusion of angular spirals and other interlocking geometric motifs. In a radical shift, textiles had moved from stylization into abstraction. These textiles probably incorporated the sacred iconography of the Wari. Although we have scarcely begun the task of interpreting these woven patterns, we can assume that they were widely understood at the time of production.

On the north coast of Peru the Moche (*c.* AD 100–700) also made fine tapestries. Spectacular garments, jewellery and regal accoutrements have been found at elite burial sites including the tomb in the Lambayeque Valley of the ruler known as the 'Lord of Sipán'. The Moche created vast quantities of pottery portrait vessels: realistic in style, they provide valuable information about local customs and clothing styles.

The Chimú (*c.* AD 900–1470) followed the Moche as the dominant political power on Peru's north coast. Like so many other pre-Hispanic cultures, the Chimú devoted vast amounts of time, energy and artistry to the care and preservation of deceased ancestors. Exquisite goldwork and textiles were placed with Chimú mummy bundles. Clothing and cloth were chiefly made from cotton – white and native brown. Featherwork was a particular speciality: arranged in overlapping rows, the brilliantly coloured plumage of tropical birds covered plain-woven cloth and headdresses with shimmering designs. The Chimú also decorated textiles with fringes, beads, shells and delicately embossed ornaments of gold or silver. Chancay textiles from the central coast (*c.*1200 –1400) are noted for the delicacy of their transparent gauzes and open-weave materials, done with finely spun cotton. Chancay tombs have also yielded up knotted textiles and striking multicoloured tapestries. Motifs include felines, monkeys, pelicans, fish and other kinds of marine life.

THE INKAS

The Inkas began their rise to power after AD 1200. From Cuzco, their imperial capital in the highlands of Peru, they eventually established a vast empire – Tawantinsuyu, 'land of the four quarters'. At its height (1438–1532), the empire took in modern Peru and Ecuador, the south of Colombia, highland Bolivia, northern Chile and northwestern Argentina; distant parts were linked by an elaborate system of roads. As latecomers, the Inkas were able to draw on the textile skills of preceding cultures. Our understanding of Inka clothing styles, cloth-making skills and ritual customs is informed by Inka burials – many at extremely high altitudes – and also by Spanish accounts from the post-conquest period. Of huge importance is the Andean manuscript of Guamán Poma de Ayala (*c.* 1535–1615). His lengthy letter to the King of Spain was accompanied by nearly four hundred pen-and-ink drawings.

In each Inka household women made cloth for their family's needs and for the tribute required by the State. Luxury cloth was produced by specialist male weavers and by 'chosen' women living in special enclosed societies.

Inka garments were unfitted and constructed from webs of uncut cloth. Women wore a wrap-around ankle-length dress: pinned over the shoulders, it was tied at the waist by a patterned belt. They used a mantle, pinned over the chest, and a cloth or band for the head. Men's dress consisted of a loincloth, tunic, rectangular mantle, bag, sandals and headdress. Clothing indicated the wearer's cultural origins and social role, with the most prestigious garments reserved for the Inka nobility. Sumptuary laws restricted the use of featherwork, *qompi* (finely spun camelid-fibre cloth, woven with an unusually high thread count), gold, silver and gemstones. Non-representational design motifs (*t'oqapu*) were similarly controlled: small rectangular pattern units, colourfully arranged in regular rows, covered the tapestry tunics of the ruler and his elite. Another style of Inka tunic displayed a bold black-and-white chequerboard pattern with a stepped red yoke; this high-status garment probably had military associations. Textiles marked life-cycle events such as births, puberty celebrations, marriages and death. The preserved mummies of royal ancestors, richly clothed and cared for in death by their attendants, were arrayed in their full finery on important feast days and carried in litters through the streets of Cuzco.

AFTER THE CONQUEST

After the traumatic conquest of Tawantinsuyu, Spanish settlers introduced sheep into the Andes together with the European treadle loom. Newly trained Andean weavers (largely male and often conscripted) produced cloth for commercial enterprises. Quality weavings increasingly combined European and oriental designs with pre-Hispanic motifs. Surviving tapestry-woven textiles from the colonial period show Inka nobles in indigenous dress with European additions such as knee breeches. Although ordinary men and women in indigenous communities were initially forbidden to wear European-style clothing, subsequent laws outlawed 'native' dress and imposed Spanish clothing styles.

Modern indigenous dress combines colonial garment styles from Spain with survivals from the pre-conquest era. These include the woman's *manta* (shawl), carrying cloths, belts for men and women, and bags for the coca leaves that combat the effects of high altitude. The man's pre-Hispanic mantle and tunic have been replaced by the *poncho*. Recent years have seen a resurgence of

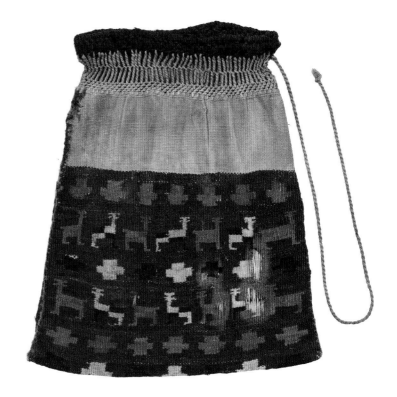

Provincial Inka-style bag made of cotton and camelid fibre in plain weave and tapestry; looping at the opening. 25 x 21.5 cm (10 x 8 1/2 in).

interest in natural dyes and traditional weaving methods in Bolivia and Peru. As in the distant past, textiles are treasured possessions that play a vital role in the lives of makers and wearers.

The Andean region has what may be the longest continuous textile record in the world. The archaeological examples seen here were a revered part of the ancient cultures they represent. With their astonishing virtuosity and vast range of designs, Andean textiles encompassed nearly every known technique. 'Encoded' with cultural information, they were a vital part of the visual language of the Andes.

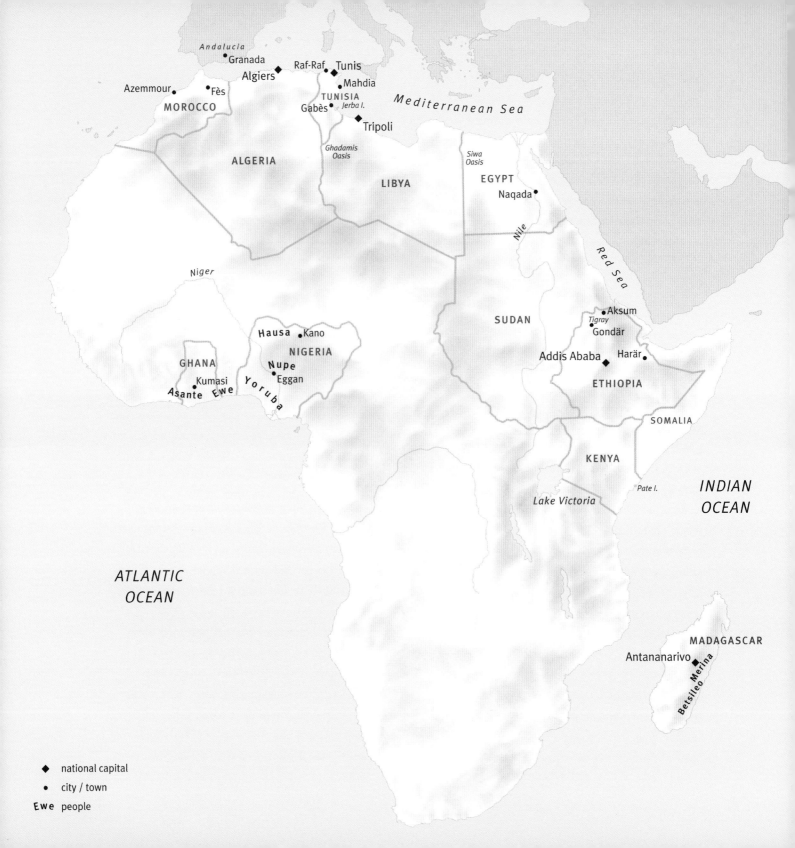

Andalucia
• Granada   Raf-Raf ◆ ◆ Tunis
Algiers ◆   ● Mahdia
Azemmour ●   ● Fès   **TUNISIA**
MOROCCO   Gabès ● *Jerba I.*

Mediterranean Sea

ALGERIA   Tripoli ◆

                    Ghadamis Oasis   *Siwa Oasis*

                              LIBYA   **EGYPT**
                                                  Naqada ●

Niger   *Nile*

                                                            Red Sea

                                    SUDAN   ● Aksum
                                                      Tigray
Hausa ● Kano   ● Gondär
          NIGERIA   Addis Ababa ◆   Harär ●
GHANA **Nupe**   **ETHIOPIA**
      ● Kumasi ● Eggan
Asante **Ewe** **Yoruba**

                                                      SOMALIA

                                          KENYA

                                    Pate I.   **INDIAN OCEAN**

                              Lake Victoria

ATLANTIC OCEAN

                                                      MADAGASCAR
                                          Antananarivo ◆ *Merina*
                                                      Betsileo

◆ national capital

● city / town

Ewe people

SILK IN AFRICA

Silk is a prestigious material, often used to produce textiles and clothing associated with wealth and social status. In Africa silk is produced and used less extensively than cotton or wool – both geographically and socially. The textiles featured here come from North Africa (Morocco, Algeria, Tunisia, Libya and Egypt), Ethiopia, West Africa (mainly Ghana and Nigeria) and Madagascar.

Some of the earliest written records of indigenous silk production in Africa come from Tunisia. We know from the writings of Ibn Hawqal, the tenth-century geographer, that the industry flourished in Gabes – the mulberry trees cultivated there were almost certainly used to raise the *Bombyx mori* (literally 'mulberry cocoon') silkworm. Raw silk was probably obtained by heating the cocoons to soften the gum binding the filaments, then reeling (unwinding) the threads directly from two or more cocoons at a time to form a continuous even strand.

As well as cultivated production several varieties of wild silk are known in Africa. In the highlands of Madagascar the indigenous *Borocera Madagascariensis* produces a coarse greyish-brown silk which resists dye. The savannah region of northern Nigeria is home to two varieties of wild silk collected from the cocoons of the *Anaphe infracta* and *Anaphe moloneyi* genus moths.

The trans-Saharan trade routes provided a vital source of silk yarn and manufactured silk cloths. Magenta waste silk, known in Nigeria as *alharini* (derived from *harir*, the Arabic word for silk), originally came from Tunisia as a by-product of the local silk industry. Later unwrought silk from French and Italian mills was imported into Gabes and Tunis and subsequently traded to Kano.

The Asante people of Ghana exploited other sources to obtain silk. By the 1730s manufactured silk or composite cloths, acquired from Europe as diplomatic gifts or via the West African coastal trade, were being unravelled for their yarn. This practice continued until the early twentieth century. Similarly, silk weavers in Ethiopia first obtained their supplies of silk yarn from unravelled imported textiles.

NORTH AFRICA

In North Africa, after the Arab invasion of the seventh century, weaving became a male profession. Factories were established to produce luxurious silk garments for the rulers and the Muslim elite. Textiles were included as tribute items or presented as gifts and rewards, particularly under the hedonistic Fatimids (909–1171) in Egypt and Tunisia. By the twelfth century specialist silk weaving guilds had been set up in Tunis. Production also flourished in Fès in Morocco.

Silk weaving, found predominantly in towns and cities, relied after the sixteenth century on various types of treadle loom. In Fès the large draw loom was used to produce intricately patterned silk textiles. The decoration and the manufacture of belts mirrored the complex dissemination of weaving techniques and ideas, as successive waves of refugees introduced technical and stylistic innovations.

Flat-woven silk textiles, often incorporating

simple stripes or checks, were made on hand-operated treadle looms in Libya, Tunisia and Egypt. The introduction of the flying shuttle to treadle looms, which the weaver operates by pulling on a short cord, allowed broader cloth widths and increased output. Today, on Jerba island and in Mahdia, Tunisia, this technique is used to create silk cloths by inserting numerous supplementary shed sticks through the warp; subtle designs, featuring elaborate geometric motifs, are often produced in two tones.

Embroidery in North Africa is a female activity. Distinctive regional styles and techniques evolved, reflecting different external influences. Amongst the finest urban embroideries are those worked on linen from Algiers. Beautiful hangings and curtains, covered with exuberant floral and vegetal designs, were produced by women for the bridal trousseau. A more formal embroidery style was adopted in Fès for cloths designed as home furnishings. Rural embroidery communicates cultural beliefs in an exuberant and engaging manner. Patterns reflect concerns about fertility, generate community well-being and protect against the evil eye. During wedding ceremonies the Tunisian women of El-Jem wear wrap-around wool cloths (*hram nfasiy*) worked in brilliantly coloured silks with striking solar and lunar motifs. Solar-inspired designs on black-and-white wedding dresses from Siwa Oasis in Egypt are also thought to have protective qualities.

ETHIOPIA

Silk has played an important role in the social and religious life of Ethiopia from the earliest days of the kingdom of Aksum, which converted to Christianity in the fourth century. It was imported in large quantities from India, Arabia and China: stored in vast caverns in the central highlands of Ethiopia, silk was used to make ceremonial umbrellas, to bind sacred books, to cover wooden altar tablets and to weave the imposing hangings that were an essential feature of Ethiopian churches. One of these spectacular hangings survives in the collection of the British Museum. Made in the mid-eighteenth century, probably by a guild of Muslim or Jewish weavers, it is the largest tablet-woven textile in the world (see page 322).

During the nineteenth century a succession of enlightened rulers began to unify the Christian empire of Ethiopia. In common with the Asante of Ghana and the Merina of Madagascar, the complex hierarchy of religious, secular and military officialdom in this empire needed delineation. An impressive range of woven or embroidered silk costumes evolved to define the status of the wearer. One such textile was the *shamma*, a toga-like cotton shawl worn throughout Ethiopia by men and women. Information about the wearer's status is conveyed even today by pattern and by the way the *shamma* is draped or folded. During the nineteenth century the honorific lion-skin cape was gradually replaced by the *lamd* – a richly decorated cape embroidered by guilds of Armenian craftsmen and worn by clerics, nobles and high-ranking military. The *kamis*, which takes

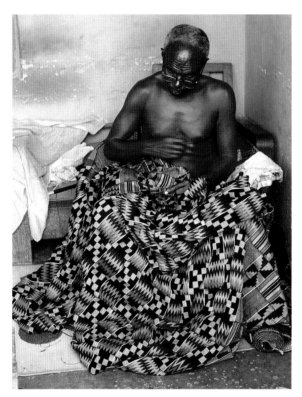

The design on this Asante textile is called 'Fathia Nkrumah' commemorating the Egyptian wife of the former president Kwame Nkruhmah, Bonwire, Ghana.

its name from the French word 'chemise', developed from the silk-embroidered tunic worn by nineteenth-century noblewomen. Similar dresses are worn today by a larger number of women, yet they remain a symbol of status.

Apart from some isolated, historical traditions such as on Pate island off the Kenyan coast, Ethiopia has long been the only major silk weaving region in eastern Africa. The Ethiopian textiles described so far, from the northern and central highlands, are predominantly Christian. Yet silk also had great significance within the ancient emirate of Harar, close to the border with Somalia

in the east: with its strong Muslim population and culture, the region was renowned for its textiles.

WEST AFRICA

In West Africa silk weaving developed as a specialist activity in Egga (modern Eggan) and surrounding Nupe towns in northern Nigeria. Distinctive cloths, made for export, were renowned as far away as Timbuktu. Yoruba, Nupe and Hausa weavers are most closely associated with the production of silk or cotton and silk strips. Among the most prestigious cloths are those made for men's robes that use the local *Anaphe infracta* silk, usually with cotton.

In early Islamic society gifts of clothing were presented to officials or members of the court to reward service and loyalty. Similarly, in the early nineteenth century, elaborately embroidered men's gowns became popular among the ruling Muslim elite of the northern Nigerian emirates. The gowns were a symbol of political and religious affiliation.

The patterns that characterize northern Nigerian gowns are formal and consistent. Specialized artisans are responsible for the separate stages or elements of manufacture, and Islamic scholars draw the preliminary designs on the cloth for the embroidery. The most distinctive design motifs are 'two knives' (*aska biyu*) and 'eight knives' (*aska takwas*). Their name and form – long triangular elements arranged in groups of two and three – suggest a protective function.

In Ghana the production of silk textiles is dominated by the Asante and the Ewe people. Their textiles are distinguished by their use of colour, and complex weft-float patterning.

Two of the most prestigious types of regalia associated with the Asante royal court were gold artefacts and silk textiles. Bonwire was the major centre of silk weaving. The *Asantehene* (the king) commissioned cloths for his exclusive use and maintained a monopoly on certain patterns. Early cotton cloths with simple, solid colour weft blocks in silk were known as *bankuo*. Gradually more complex finely banded weft blocks (*babadua*) were introduced: these were eventually combined with intricate weft-float designs (*adwin*) and incorporated geometric patterns such as triangles, zigzags and lozenges. Sumptuous silk cloths (*asasia*) with intricate weft-inlay designs were made exclusively for the *Asantehene*.

The Ewe people did not have a strong centralized government or court, so there was no monopoly of silk cloth production. Ewe cloths could be acquired by anyone with sufficient financial means and were commissioned for specific occasions such as marriage, the birth of a child, funerals or special festivals. The most prestigious type of Ewe cloth is the *adanudo* which can be woven of high-quality cotton but is more usually produced in silk or a silk and rayon mix. The patterns on older cloths are highly stylized, but recent examples are more naturalistic and explicit in their use of images.

MADAGASCAR

Madagascar's different textile traditions reflect the numerous waves of people who have settled on the island over the centuries. The most prestigious

of these textiles have been made of silk. Associated with royalty and immortality, silk is woven today by the Merina and Betsileo people. Until recently all weaving was undertaken by women. Although *lamba* is a generic name for all cloth in Madagascar, it has come to describe the shawl that is worn by Malagasy men and women, rich and poor.

Shrouds (*lamba mena*), woven from the durable greyish-brown thread provided by indigenous silkworm, are the most expensive of all Malagasy textiles. During elaborate 'second-burial' rituals (*famadihana*) – which, like much else in Malagasy culture, has its origins in Indonesia – the dead are wrapped in an additional shroud of elaborately patterned silk cloth (*lamba akotofahana*).

Although most Malagasy textiles express their predominant design in the warp, weft-float patterns became an increasingly important feature of Merina textiles during the nineteenth century. Some patterns are derived from trees and flowers – these probably relate to the system of honours that helped to define the hierarchy of the Merina kingdom in the nineteenth century.

Colours added a further dimension to the significance of cloth. Malagasy colour symbolism is extremely subtle. Green is associated with mourning, and the term *lamba maitso* (literally 'green cloth') is one of the terms used to describe mourning cloth, though green may not be its actual colour. Similarly *lamba mena* (literally 'red cloth') is a term used to describe the shrouds used for burying the dead, though they are not necessarily red in colour. The colour red had been associated for centuries with royalty (who among the Merina were thought to be immortal), vitality and mystical power. The cloth became so closely identified with what red represented that when the colours changed, the name did not.

TRADITION AND CHANGE

Africa's textile traditions are threatened by mechanization, imported goods, changing social structures and modern fashions. As some traditions decline, however, others take their place. Throughout the continent there is probably more distinctively African cloth being manufactured today than at any other time. Silk textiles have always been associated with status – with aristocracy and royalty, with ancestors and even with deities. Today there is still a demand for prestigious, culturally significant cloths. These glamorous textiles are less exposed to competition from imported goods than everyday, utilitarian fabrics. On the other hand, silk weaving traditions may be more vulnerable to sudden social or political change. When the Malagasy monarchy and the Merina kingdom lost power and authority during the colonial period, the significance of the colour and patterning of the *lamba akotofahana* dwindled. In modern times, however, silk weavers in both Tunisia and Madagascar are continuing to meet the local demand for cloth while also experimenting with designs and patterns not used since the nineteenth century. In Ethiopia, meanwhile, weavers are producing more *shamma* than ever before. In West Africa the silk *kente* cloth of the Asante (now frequently woven in rayon) is worn by a widening cross-section of Ghanaian

Weavers in the town of Arivonimamo, Madagascar use specially adapted looms to reproduce the brightly coloured silk textiles that were once exclusively worn by the Merina nobility.

society, often replacing suits and ties for formal occasions. Textiles from the old silk weaving town of Naqada in Egypt's Nile Valley – woven increasingly by women – are sold in shops around the world. In their different ways, the silk textiles featured here continue to encapsulate the enduring dynamism and versatility of so many textile traditions throughout Africa.

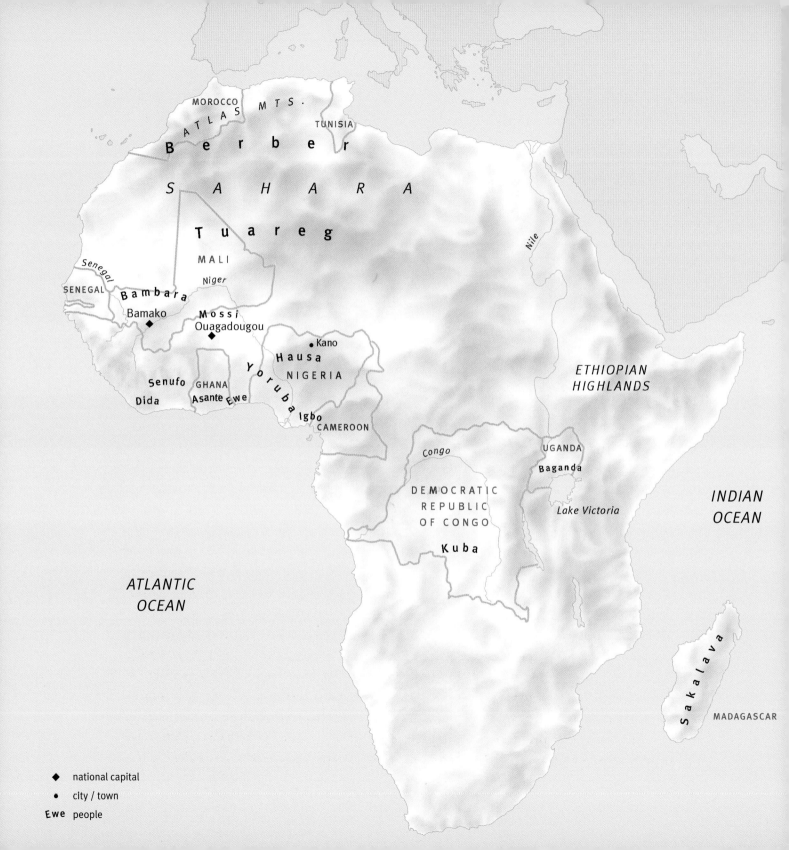

MOROCCO

ATLAS MTS.

TUNISIA

B e r b e r

S A H A R A

T u a r e g

MALI

Senegal

SENEGAL

Niger

Bambara

Bamako

Mossi

Ouagadougou

Kano

Hausa

NIGERIA

Senufo

GHANA

Yoruba

Dida

Asante Ewe

Igbo

CAMEROON

Nile

ETHIOPIAN
HIGHLANDS

Congo

UGANDA

Baganda

DEMOCRATIC
REPUBLIC
OF CONGO

Kuba

Lake Victoria

INDIAN
OCEAN

ATLANTIC
OCEAN

S a k a l a v a

MADAGASCAR

◆ national capital

• city / town

Ewe people

PRINTED AND DYED TEXTILES FROM AFRICA

Africa has long held a fascination for those born outside this great continent. Over the centuries its wealth of minerals, animal products and manpower has drawn in colonists and traders, slavers and missionaries alike. Its huge population is of diverse origin: people of Arab and Berber descent in the north, Khoisan-speakers and European colonists in the extreme south, Nilotic-speaking peoples in the north-east, and south of the Sahara a rich mix of groups who speak one of the Bantu languages. Although African textile traditions attracted little foreign academic interest until the twentieth century, African textiles began to enter European collections well before 1900.

Trade is central to the story of African textiles. To go to any market in West Africa is to see women swathed in brightly patterned wraps – usually wax-printed factory-made batiks of Dutch or local origin. European wax prints, based on Javanese batik, are an important trade item throughout sub-Saharan Africa. Damasks from China and Europe are another major import – it is on these and locally made damasks that tied-resist indigo-dyeing is often done. Yet despite the availability of imported textiles, large amounts of cloth are still woven at home.

Traditionally, West African cloths are made from long, narrow strips of fabric, cut into appropriate lengths and sewn together selvedge to selvedge. Rolls of this cloth once served as currency in place of money. Before the colonial period, barkcloth was widely used in central and parts of East Africa. People who were not subject to Muslim influence went naked or wrapped a simple piece of reddish-brown barkcloth around the waist or loins. The African way of beating the inner bark of fig trees to make cloth is similar to that used in Polynesia.

RAPHIA

Raphia, once used extensively as a weaving material, remains an important textile fibre in parts of the Congo, Angola and the island of Madagascar. Translucent fibres are extracted from the young leaves of *Raphia ruffia* or *R. taedigiria* (palm trees native to Madagascar) and dried in the sun to produce silken strands about a metre (3 ft) long. The name 'raphia' is probably derived from the Malagasy word *rofia*.

The highlands of Madagascar are inhabited by tribes of Malay descent, who reached the island in the first millennium after a long sea voyage from what is now Indonesia; coastal regions have mixed populations, with a black African element. The textile tradition in Madagascar shares distinctive features with that of South East Asia. Although most Malagasy raphia textiles are undyed and naturally beige, warp-*ikat* decorated cloths are made in three highland villages by the Sakalava, who use a technique closely associated with the Indonesian islands. Today warp threads are tied and dipped in a single dye bath to achieve simple, two-colour patterns in the woven cloth. In the past, however, when more than one dye bath was used, textiles were patterned in several colours with human figures and geometric devices. Warp-*ikat* is also practised in Nigeria by the Yoruba, who incorporate it into strip weaves or women's vertical-loom cloths in longitudinal stripes to add contrasting detail.

The Kuba – a tribal confederation based along the Kasai river in the Congo – work in wood, metal and raphia. Often described as the finest artists in Africa, they were highly resistant to the colonial trade in cotton cloth. Male weavers produce raphia cloth on a single-heddle overhead loom: the length of strands limits the size of fabric to one metre (3 ft) square. The raphia textile repertoire of the Kuba includes squares or rectangles of cloth and long dance skirts for both men and women. Skirts are made from six or more panels: these are sewn together and embellished with embroidery, cut-pile, pierced work, patchwork or appliqué; cowrie shells and bobbled borders are sometimes added. Styles of decoration are indicative of social status, gender and tribal affiliations. Some skirt-makers tie or stitch in a resist before dyeing: deep browns and reds are obtained using locally available materials such as camwood, brimstone, or mud and charcoal.

INDIGO

Indigo dyeing is widespread throughout West Africa, in areas where there is an abundance of indigo-bearing plants and in locations that are on major trade routes. The ancient city of Kano in northern Nigeria was for centuries one of the main termini of the caravan trails from the Maghreb across the Sahara and down to West Africa. In pre-industrial times Kano was famous for its indigo-dyed cloth. Today, however, this cloth has been largely replaced by mill-made materials and factory-sewn clothing, while natural indigo has been superseded by synthetic dyes of many hues. Nevertheless, Kano's Kofor Mata dye pits are still in operation after more than 500 years. Male dyers mix natural indigo with wood ash and potassium soda steeped in water. Indigo is a substantive dye so needs no mordant, but it has to be fermented and deoxidized in an alkaline solution to convert the indican (the active dyeing agent) into a soluble form that can be absorbed into the fibres. Cloth is repeatedly exposed to the air during dyeing. All kinds of cloth are dyed in Kano: hand-woven plain cloth, cloth with a resist – even jeans. Resist-dyed cloth production is confined to rather crude tie-and-dye and some stitched resist. The tying, generally done by women, consists of simply tying knots into the cloth in concentric circles. Cloth is left to soak in the dye bath, then lifted out for 30–45 seconds. This process is repeated until the desired shade is achieved: light blue takes an hour and a half of dipping and aerating, navy blue three hours, light black four hours, and deep blue-black six hours.

Three main ethnic groups predominate in Nigeria, the most populous country in Africa: the Yoruba in the south-west, the Igbo in the south-east and the Hausa in the north. All have a strong indigo-dyeing tradition (as do many smaller Nigerian tribal groupings), but it is most

Dyeing with indigo at the Kofor Mata dye pits in Kano, Nigeria.

prevalent among the Yoruba. Abeokuta, Oshogbo, Ede and formerly Ibadan in Yorubaland are all famed for their indigo dyeing. Master-dyers in Yorubaland use indigo to achieve intense blue-black shades, but like to keep their methods secret from inquisitive outsiders.

Indigo-dyeing is also done in St Louis, Kaedi and Kayes, all situated on the Senegal river, which wends its way down from Mali through Mauretania and Senegal. Some centres have a tradition of elaborate pattern dyeing, while others restrict themselves to simple designs or none at all. Indigo has always been the most popular natural dye: the plants are readily available, and it has the great advantage that it dyes cold. However, it is not the only dye produced from natural sources. Crushed cola nuts from the *Cola nitida* tree give a golden brown, while cassava roots yield a natural red dye called *alari*, also said to be obtainable from husks of guinea corn (millet or sorghum).

TIE-DYING

Regardless of the dye used, methods for tie-dyeing cloth are similar everywhere. The Dida live in Côte d'Ivoire. For ceremonial occasions Dida women plait strands of raphia to make tubular skirts, cloaks and kerchiefs. These are patterned by means of tied resist. Designs include circles, ovals and rectangles, often combined with distinct areas of dots. Dyes are obtained from natural sources: red and black on a yellowish ground is a popular combination. Garments are dyed from the lightest colour to the darkest.

The most colourful of all African tie-dyed textiles are the rectangular shoulder-cloths of southern Tunisia. Formerly made in the village of Matmata but now mainly in Chenini de Gabes, they are worn by Berber women to protect their clothes from the oil that they put on their hair. Small bundles of wheat grains are tied into the woollen fabric, and tasselled borders are embellished with lines of cotton stitching. Cloths are dipped into different dye baths: whereas wool rapidly absorbs the colour, the cotton stitching remains white. This exploitation of the difference in dye take-up between wool and cotton finds its highest expression in the *bakhnug* (shawls) of Berber women near Tataouine. Woollen fabric is patterned on the loom with cotton supplementary wefts. After dyeing, the cotton details retain their original colour, in sharp contrast to the deep background colour. In Morocco tie-dyed veils are worn by Ayt Atta and Djeballa Berber women. Small stones or woodchips, knotted into thickish woollen cloth, create large isolated designs. The fabric is usually dyed only once, the most common colour combinations being black or light blue against a red background, or red or brown against yellow.

Simple tie-dyed cloths are used as food covers in Morocco, Algeria and Libya, as women's belts in Morocco and Tunisia, and as women's head coverings in Morocco and Tunisia. More complex work decorated in a spiral of little dots can be found at Garian in Libya, but this is sometimes worked on finer, imported fabric. Mauretania has a tradition of fine tie-dyed multicoloured shawls of thin muslin. Throughout Africa tying may be done by pinching up the fabric and tying it off with raphia or cotton thread. It is also common, as described, to insert small objects such as pebbles or buttons into the ties.

STITCH RESIST

Stitch resist, much used throughout Africa, also enables dyers to 'reserve' selected areas of cloth. In Burkina Faso blue waist and chest wraps, patterned with rows of white arrow designs, are sold by the market vendors of Ouagadougou. The base cloth, like much hand-woven fabric in West Africa, is formed by eight or ten narrow strips, sewn selvedge to selvedge. The strips are made by itinerant weavers, who carry their portable looms from family courtyard to family courtyard. They receive food and a present every day, and a parting gift such as a goat when their task is complete.

In the north of Burkina Faso women of the Mossi tribe create symmetrical patterning by tightly sewing arrowhead designs into folded cloth. Raphia thread is preferred to cotton, because it is tougher. When the thread is pulled tight, stitched areas in the compressed fabric become impervious to dye. The Mossi grow *Indigofera tinctoria* and *Lonchocarpus cyanescus*, the main indigo-bearing plants. Cloth is dyed in deep, lidded pits in the ground. When the desired deep blue has been achieved – which may take many dippings – the raphia threads are removed to reveal the resist pattern.

Similar cloths are created – by this method and variations of it – throughout West Africa, from Senegambia in the north to Cameroon in

Tying resists into leather at Oshogbo in Yorubaland, Nigeria.

the south. Most stitch resist is blue (although synthetic indigo has replaced natural indigo in many places) or cola-nut brown. In Nigeria, Gambia, Senegal, Mali and other parts of West Africa, stitch-resist textiles are produced by machine sewing as well as by hand. Originally the machine stitching was done by male tailors, but today – as the demands of commerce increasingly break down occupational barriers between the sexes – it is often women who carry out this work, particularly in Nigeria.

Imports of European mill cloth and smooth sewing threads have increased the delicacy of much stitch-resist work, but the finest examples were made before the Second World War in St Louis, in northern Senegal. European mill-woven cloth was folded and pleated, then sewn with cotton thread in patterns so intricate as to merit being called embroidery. After dyeing in indigo, the thread resists were painstakingly unpicked to reveal Moorish-inspired patterns, probably derived from nearby Mauretania. This tradition has been revived to suit modern Senegalese tastes.

In Nigeria the Igbo of northern Igboland produce splendid stitch-resist pictorial cloths known as *ukura*. Traditionally made for the Leopard Society of Cross River in the extreme south-east of Nigeria, *ukura* often feature leopard and other animal motifs rich with symbolism.

Adire is the Yoruba word for resist dyeing with indigo. Tie-dyed cloth is known as *adire oniko*, a term derived from the Yoruba word for raphia, and stitched resist as *adire alabere*, from the word meaning stitch. With *adire alabere*,

cloth is folded or pleated (sometimes longitudinally or diagonally) and hand-stitched with raphia thread or machine-sewn with cotton to create carefully organized repeat designs. Although hand-stitching is traditionally done by women and machine sewing by men, such gender differentiations are becoming increasingly blurred. The term *etu* (the Yoruba name for the guinea fowl pattern) can be applied to any textile design reminiscent of the speckled plumage of this bird. The Yoruba produce beautiful tied-resist and stitch-resist *etu* cloths in square and circular patterns: these are so pleasing to the eye that they are often not untied or unstitched.

Starch resist, or *adire eleko*, is another Yoruba speciality. With this technique, cassava or cornflour starch (*lafun*) is mixed with alum and applied to one side of the cloth. This resist medium works well with indigo, because the low temperature of the dye-vat will not dissolve the starch. An image of King George V and Queen Mary at their silver jubilee in 1935 is one of the many designs that have been used on *adire* cloths. In Ibadan, as in the distant past, women apply the starch with a palm-rib or bird's feather quill. Production is labour-intensive and extremely slow. Patterns are mostly traditional: first a grid is drawn in *lafun*, then the squares are filled in with a range of motifs. Stencilling, found today in Abeokuta, is a faster process that probably started in the late nineteenth century. Stencils, once made from the linings of tea chests or cigar boxes, are now chiselled out of 30 x 20 cm (12 x 8 in) rectangles of zinc. Cloth is nailed to a worktable, and the *lafun* is pressed through the stencils with a metal spatula; when the dyeing is complete, the *lafun* is scraped off the cloth. Most cloths require a series of stencils: these are used in descending order of importance to the design. Although stencilling was formerly a male task, the situation is changing.

Wax, easier to apply and stronger than starch resists, is used – often in conjunction with synthetic dyes – throughout Africa. Dyers dip a sponge into molten wax and squeeze it by hand on to the cloth; the wax is later boiled out of the cloth. Most of the variations seen in traditional and modern batik in other parts of the world are also to be found in Africa. The crumpling of the wax resist before dyeing to create a crackled effect in the finished cloth has a history that stretches back at least to the nineteenth century. Among the young, a brightly coloured 'psychedelic' look is currently popular.

Clamp-resist dyeing, although associated principally with Japan, is used to a limited extent in West Africa. With this technique, cloth is pleated and compressed into a cube; when it is dipped in the dye-bath, the outer edges absorb the colour, while the clamped or 'reserved' squares remain the original base colour.

ADINKRA

Ghana is one of the few countries in sub-Saharan Africa where cloth is block-printed (another notable instance being in Sierra Leone). In the village of Ntonso, close to Bonwire (the centre of Asante weaving), *adinkra* cloth is hand-stamped with moons, ferns and other symbolic designs carved into the hard outer surface of calabash gourds. The printers – mostly elderly men, because few young men want such poorly paid work – start by drawing a grid on Chinese factory-made cloth. By repeatedly rolling their curved calabash stamps, they apply rows of design motifs to all the squares of the grid. Each man completes about two *adinkra* cloths a day: these are hung out overnight to catch the dew. In Ghana dark clothing is required for funerals. Some mourners use a black infusion of badee tree-bark to obliterate the bright colours of strip-weave *kente* cloth, but traditionally minded mourners commission a block-printed wrap of *adinkra* cloth, overdyed with red or black, to indicate grief.

MUDCLOTH

The *bogolanfini*, or 'mud cloths', of Mali are among the most striking of all African textiles. Decorated with geometric patterns in white on black, they are hand-woven by Bamana/Bambara women to the north of Bamako (Mali's capital). Although they have become a fashion item – not just within Mali but across Africa and beyond – they were used originally as hunters' shirts and women's wraps. Contrary to appearances, cloth is not resist-dyed. Instead makers soak their strip-woven fabrics in a tannin-rich mulch of leaves from local trees. The tannin turns the cloth yellow, but also serves as a mordant to fix the black colour of the river mud that is applied to the cloth.

Pattern areas are restored to white when makers bleach them using millet bran and peanuts.

PAINTED CLOTHS

In Africa painted cloths have a talismanic significance. Since the very beginning of Islam, written quotations from the Koran or the Hadiths have been thought to have protective powers. With progressive Islamicization, the Muslim custom of inscribing Arabic invocations on clothing spread down into black Africa from Arabia, Asia and North Africa. Shirts bearing Arabic calligraphy were greatly prized by tribal warriors. The famous Hausa trading city of Kano developed as a major centre for their production and distribution; from there Hausa craftsmen moved on to other parts of West Africa, where they made similarly inscribed cloths – not just for Islamic groups, but also for non-Islamic groups such as the Asante. With their strong warrior tradition, the Asante were happy to adopt an Islamic custom that celebrated valour.

THE FUTURE

Recent years have seen the spread of factory-made cloth, bought for its bright colours, washability, and ease of tailoring into Western-style clothing. Yet two important factors have helped to preserve the legacy of hand-crafted cloth-making. Throughout Africa traditional garments are still regarded as essential for ceremonies marking 'rites of passage', and for funerals in particular. In the West, meanwhile, African textiles are increasingly admired. This, in turn, influences the fashion tastes of Africa's urban elite. As long as a discerning local market exists, traditional weavers, dyers and embroiders will continue to meet that demand, patterning fine cloth and keeping African textile traditions alive for the foreseeable future.

chapter 1

Textiles from the Balkans

Detail from a woman's chemise, with stylized motifs in orange and black embroidery (in wool). A later generation would have added the sequins and beadwork. Bitola region, Former Yugoslav Republic of Macedonia, mid-20th century. 127 x 105 cm (50 x 41^1/$_2$ in). Given by Ken Ward.

TRIBAL SLIPPERS
Northern Albania, 1912

Edith Durham records receiving these hand-knitted slippers
from Gruda tribesmen in the mountainous area of North Albania
in 1912, in return for aid to burnt-out villages'. Durham was one
of the great women travellers in the Balkans in the early 1900s.
Her *High Albania*, published in 1909, remains a standard text to
this day. Made of hand-spun wool, these slippers are decorated
with commercial black braiding at the top, with a large applied
motif with couched gold-coloured metal-wrapped thread.
33 × 16 cm (13¼ × 6½ in)
Given by Mary Edith Durham

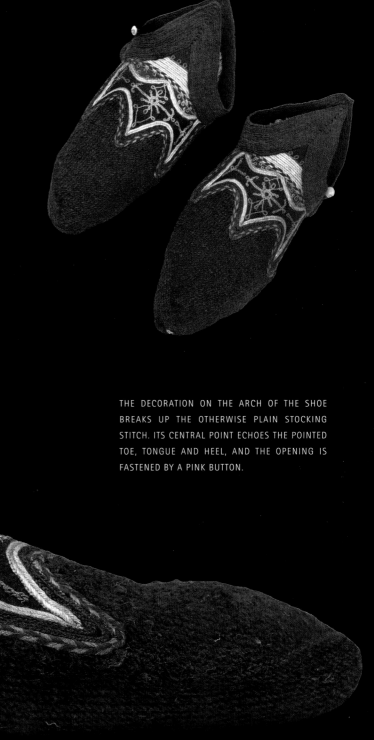

THE DECORATION ON THE ARCH OF THE SHOE
BREAKS UP THE OTHERWISE PLAIN STOCKING
STITCH. ITS CENTRAL POINT ECHOES THE POINTED
TOE, TONGUE AND HEEL, AND THE OPENING IS
FASTENED BY A PINK BUTTON.

WOMAN'S HEADBAND
Albania, early 20th century

Women's headbands were worn vertically. They
have a pointed end at the bottom and the top is
raised and stiffened with paper. Here, a pink
cotton velvet ground fabric is decorated with 'S',
'C' and flower-shaped motifs.
64 × 9.5 cm (25¼ × 3¾ in)
Acquired from Mrs J.G. Davis

THE MOTIFS ARE WORKED WITH COUCHED GOLD- AND SILVER-COLOURED METAL-WRAPPED THREAD,
BRASS SEQUINS AND A FEW PURPLE AND GREEN SEQUINS.

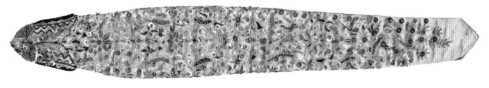

WOMAN'S HEADBAND
Albania, early 20th century

A lemon yellow satin silk ground is heavily decorated with couched embroidery and brass sequins with small coral beads attached. The headband is lined with two yellow fabrics: a golden yellow silk damask with a stemmed flower pattern, and a plain lemon yellow twill fabric.

64 × 9.5 cm (25 1/4 × 3 3/4 in)

Acquired from Mrs J. G. Davis

DAISY-LIKE FLOWERS, TULIPS AND OTHER FOLIATE SHAPES ARE WORKED IN COUCHED GOLD-COLOURED METAL-WRAPPED THREAD AND GREEN, BLUE, PINK, RED AND PURPLE SILK EMBROIDERY.

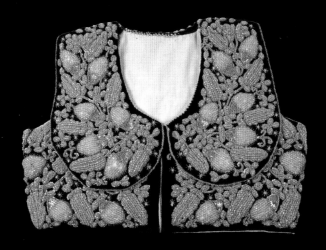

DEEP RED COTTON VELVET IS COVERED IN PARTLY PADDED EMBROIDERY AND ELABORATE COUCHING.

THE FLOWER AND LEAF MOTIFS ARE WORKED IN PALE PINK PEARLS, SEQUINS AND GOLD-COLOURED BRAIDING.

WEDDING WAISTCOAT
Albania, early 20th century

This Albanian woman's waistcoat is part of an urban Muslim wedding outfit, which includes trousers, a wrap-around skirt, an apron, a blouse and a headcloth.
35 × 47 cm (13³/₄ × 18¹/₂ in)
Acquired from Roberto Busati

THE CUFFS AND THE COLLARS ARE DELICATELY EMBROIDERED
WITH MULTI-COLOURED SYNTHETIC WOOL AND COTTON YARNS,
WITH A CROCHETED TRIM ON THE SLEEVES.

MAN'S SHIRT (*ZADRIME*)
Albania, early 20th century

This everyday shirt is knee-length, and is made of cream and beige
striped cotton cloth. It is made up of several panels: the one for the front and
back use the full width, two for each sleeve and two for each side gusset. The wide
sleeves are set at right-angles and gathered into a deep cuff.
97×156 cm ($38^{1}/_{4} \times 61^{1}/_{2}$ in) with sleeves spread out
Given by Stephanie Schwandner

WOMAN'S OUTER GARMENT (*SUKMAN*)
Govedartsi village, Samakov district, Bulgaria, late 19th century

Made of black woollen felted cloth, this garment has a scooped
shaped neckline to reveal the embroidered chemise worn beneath.
The neckline is finely decorated with rows of multi-coloured
chain stitch and has a small separate round collar. The red sleeves
(right) are very densely decorated.
116×105 cm ($45^2/_3 \times 41^1/_3$ in)
Given by the Bulgarian Committee
for Cultural Relations

THE SLEEVES HAVE A MIXTURE OF CHAIN STITCH AND BRIGHTLY COLOURED
BRAIDING. THE MULTI-COLOURED HEM INCLUDES IMPORTED GOLD.

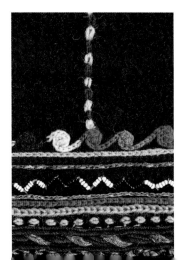

WOMAN'S OUTER JACKET
Smolyan, Bulgaria, early 20th century

Trimmed with fur and with fine couched embroidery at the
neck opening, the breast and on the cuffs, this jacket would
have been worn by a wealthy merchant's wife. The
embroidery features an endless knot and flowing motifs
based on plants – the designs are identical on each side.
39.5 × 112 cm (15 $^2/_3$ × 44 in)
Given by the Bulgarian Committee
for Cultural Relations

THE FLUID METAL-WRAPPED THREAD IS
COUCHED WITH YELLOW SILK.

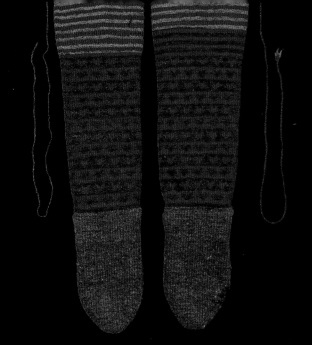

WOMAN'S SOCKS
Kyustendil, western Bulgaria,
mid-20th century

Stocking stitch is used here, with natural
coloured wools. 54 × 16 cm (21 1/4 × 6 1/3 in)
Diane Waller collection

WOMAN'S SOCKS
Velingrad, Rodopi Mountains, Bulgaria,
mid-20th century

Hand-knitted, with homespun natural
cream wool. 43.5 × 44 cm (17 1/4 × 17 1/3 in)
Given by Mercia MacDermott

WOMAN'S SOCKS
Sofia region, Bulgaria,
mid-20th century

Knitted in stocking stitch.
50 × 49.5 cm (19 2/3 × 19 1/2 i
Given by Mercia MacDermo

THESE SOCKS HAVE BEEN MADE
FROM A MIX OF COMMERCIAL
WOOLS, WHICH ARE MORE SOFTLY
SPUN, AND TIGHTER HOMESPUN
YARNS.

WOMAN'S SOCKS
Pleven, northern Bulgaria, early 20th century

Part of a woman's festive attire, these socks use
a slight variant of the western stocking stitch.
52 × 17 cm (20 1/2 × 6 2/3 in)
Given by Mrs Protitch Moreggio

WOMAN'S SOCKS
Rodopi Mountains, Bulgaria, mid-20th century

Using polychrome woollen yarns, the socks
are hand-knitted in stocking stitch.
42.5 × 15 cm (16 3/4 × 6 in)
Given by Mercia MacDermott

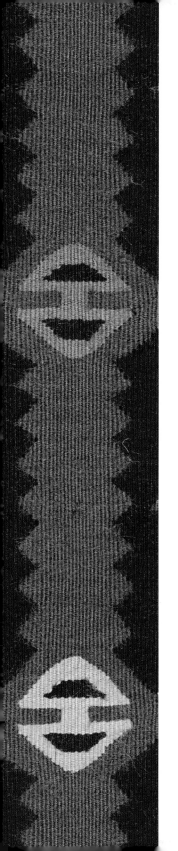

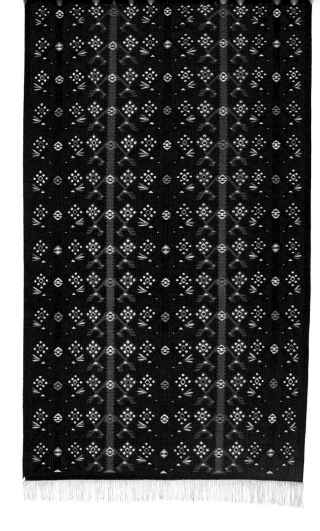

CARPET (*KILIM*)
Chiprovtsi, Bulgaria, early 20th century

The carpet is woven with five large 'tree of life' motifs,
woven on a vertical loom. The ornaments are known as trellis vine (*loznitsa*).
Two green motifs altenate with blue/black trees of life, decorated
with birds sitting above fruit or leaves.
319 × 186 cm (125²/₃ × 73¹/₄ in)
Given by the Bulgarian Committee
for Cultural Relations

THIS IS TYPICAL OF THE CHIPROVTSKI REGION. THE BRIGHTLY
COLOURED STYLIZED PLANT AND BIRD MOTIFS CONTRAST WITH
THE PLAIN BACKGROUND.

WOMAN'S SLEEVELESS COAT
Mirdita region, Albania, mid-20th century

This felted wool everyday coat would have been worn over an embroidered chemise. Made of natural, cream-coloured twill woven wool cloth, it is richly decorated on both the back and the front with couched embroidery. Although red is the predominant colour, multi-coloured yarns were used.
105 × 47 cm (41^{1}/$_{3}$ × 18^{1}/$_{2}$ in). Given by Erika Tappe

THIS MOTIF DEFINES THE SHAPE OF THE WAIST. IT IS USED ON THE LEFT AND RIGHT SIDES OF THE COAT.

MAN'S WAISTCOAT (*MEIDANI*)
Macedonia, Greece, early 20th century

This formal waistcoat would only have been worn by a wealthy person, due to the cost of its silver and gold embroidery. It would have been made from one piece of cloth by a male tailor (*terzidhes*), from the mountainous areas of Greece. Such a garment is part of a long tradition, going back to the 4th century.
29 × 40.5 cm (11¹/₂ × 16 in). Given by Dr H. P. Livas-Dawes

THE VIVID COLOURS OF THE SILK LINING COMPLEMENT THE ELABORATE EMBROIDERY AND METAL-WRAPPED THREAD.

WOMAN'S APRON
Bitola region, Former Yugoslav Republic of Macedonia,
mid-20th century

Part of a wedding outfit, the apron is made of two equal-sized pieces of
woven wool cloth joined at the centre (see above). Ribbon and rick rack,
which is made from gold-coloured metal-wrapped thread, are stitched to
the sides. The lower half of the apron is more richly decorated, and
includes coins from the region and heavy woollen fringing.
69 × 56 cm (27 × 22 in). Diane Waller collection

THE FRINGING CONSISTS OF
SEVERAL LAYERS OF SUBTLY
DIFFERENT SHADES OF RED WOOL,
INTERSPERSED WITH GOLD AND
YELLOW THREAD. THE SEQUINS
AND COINS WOULD HAVE BEEN
ADDED BY LATER GENERATIONS.

DECORATIVE TOWEL
Skopje region, Former Yugoslav Republic of Macedonia, mid-20th century

Towels such as this were usually given as gifts at a wedding
ceremony. It would have been tucked into a man's belt,
as part of his festive summer attire.
92 × 26 cm (26¹/₄ × 10¹/₄ in). Diane Waller collection

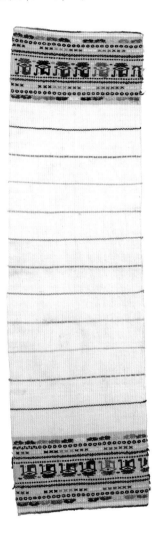

THE MULTICOLOURED GEOMETRIC MOTIFS MAY BE BASED ON BIRDS.

THE MAIN FABRIC IS A CHEQUERED
WOVEN WOOL CLOTH. THE FRONT
PANEL IS EXTREMELY ELABORATE,
INCORPORATING A MIXTURE OF
APPLIED MATERIALS.

WOMAN'S SLEEVELESS COAT
Skopje region, Former Yugoslav Republic of Macedonia,
mid-20th century

This coat would have been worn as part of a woman's festive summer attire.
It is made of woven wool cloth, which would have been purchased from travelling
merchants. Although the material is used as economically as possible,
it still achieves a very elegant silhouette.
89 × 83 cm (35 × 32²/₃ in). Diane Waller collection

WOMAN'S APRON (*FUTA*)
Skopje region, Former Yugoslav Republic of Macedonia,
mid-20th century

The apron ties pull in the material, so that when worn
the apron is gathered at the top. It is made in tapestry
weave using goat hair thread, which would have been
woven by women in the village and dyed by the men.
64×69 cm ($25^1/4 \times 27^1/4$ in)
Given by Ken Ward

AGAINST A BRILLIANT RED BACKGROUND, THE LARGE DIAMONDS CONTAIN COLOURFUL MOTIFS, WHICH ARE ALL
SLIGHTLY DIFFERENT. BLACK CHEVRONS AND WHITE ZIG-ZAGS PROVIDE A LIVELY SURROUND TO EACH DIAMOND.

IN CLUSTERS OF THE SAME
COLOUR, THE POMPOMS ARE
STITCHED TO A LACE BORDER
ALONG THE SIDES AND
HEMLINE OF THE APRON.

WOMAN'S APRON
Vevčani, near Ohrid, Former Yugoslav Republic of Macedonia, 1920s

As with the apron on pp. 98–9, the ties gather the material at the top
when the apron is worn. The colours that have been stitched onto
the main body of the apron are also used for the pompoms.
74 × 76.5 cm (29 1/4 × 30 in)
Diane Waller collection

chapter 2

Embroidery from Palestine

Detail from a veil (*khirqah*) of fine natural linen, embroidered in silk and wool in a variety of stitches. It is bordered with lace of European origin. The floral and curvilinear motifs are typical of Bethlehem embroidery although they are here employed in a more free-flowing, exuberant manner than on other garments. Bethlehem, 19th or early 20th century. 168 x 83 cm (66 x 32 $^1/_2$ in).

COAT (*JILLAYEH*)
Galilee, 19th century

The main fabric is indigo-blue cotton, with yoke and underarm inserts in rust-red cotton.
The coat is lavishly decorated with silk embroidery (see over), appliqué patches of green,
red and yellow taffeta (*heremzi*) and striped and *ikat*-dyed satins (*atlas*).
121 × 89 cm (47³/₄ × 35 in)

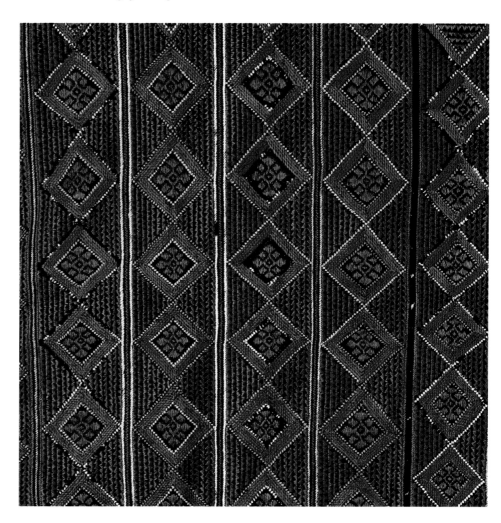

THE SILK THREAD ON THE BACK OF
THE COAT IS REMARKABLY DENSE,
AND WAS CLEARLY INTENDED TO
PROCLAIM WEALTH. THE REPEAT
PATTERN IS EXECUTED MAINLY IN
SATIN STITCH; OTHER STITCHES
INCLUDE A LINE OF DRAWN-
THREAD WORK (LEFT).

DRESS (*THOB*)
Anabta, near Nablus, *c*. 1930s

This dress is made from a locally
woven fabric called 'heaven-and-hell'
(*jinneh-u-nar*). It is of white cotton,
with green and red silk stripes at
the selvedge. The sides and sleeves
of the dress have inserts and
patches of striped and *ikat*-
patterned Syrian satin (*atlas*).
138 × 150 cm (54¹/₂ × 59 in)

THE SLEEVES ARE ATTACHED INSIDE
OUT AND WERE FOLDED BACK TO SHOW
THEIR DECORATIVE PANELS WHEN THE
DRESS WAS WORN.

DRESS (*THOB*)
Beit 'Ummar, north of Hebron, 1930s–1940s

This dress of dark blackish-blue linen has a yoke of striped satin and panels of 'royal'
(*malak*) fabric inserted in the sleeves. The embroidery is mainly in purple cross
stitch with touches of other colours. There is also some Bethlehem-style
couching on the chest panel and collar.
152 × 138 cm (60 × 54¹/₂ in)

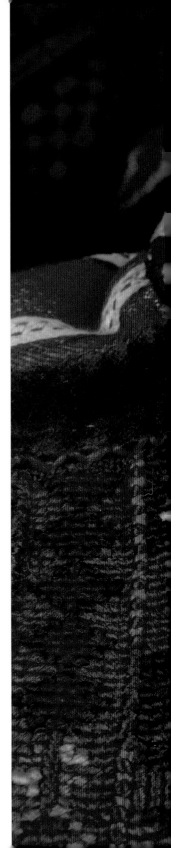

BETHLEHEM INFLUENCE IS EVIDENT IN THE BORDERS
AND ROSETTES IN METALLIC CORD COUCHING AND THE
HERRINGBONE FRAMES.

COAT-DRESS (*JILLAYEH*)
Ramallah, 19th century

The indigo linen is decorated with floss-silk embroidery,
mainly in orangey-red with touches of other colours on the skirt and chest
square. The lower part of the skirt is so densely embroidered that the
background fabric is almost entirely concealed. The predominant pattern is
the zigzag 'tall palms' motif which was, as here, usually executed in double-
sided cross stitch. This was the main symbolic marker of
Ramallah and its surrounding villages.
127 × 105 cm (50 × 41¹/₂ in)
Donated by Jerusalem and the East Mission

THE SOLID EMBROIDERY COVERING MOST OF THE SKIRT CONTRASTS
WITH THE DELICATE PATTERNS IN YELLOW, GREEN, MAUVE, WHITE AND
PINK WHICH EDGE THE SKIRT OPENING.

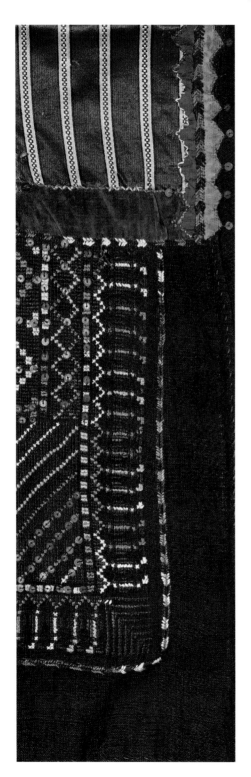

COAT-DRESS (*JILLAYEH*)
Beit Dajan, near Jaffa, *c.*1920

This was the best dress in the
bride's part of the trousseau until
after the First World War. The
opening in the front of the skirt is
patched with maroon, orange and
green taffeta (*heremzi*) and
decorated with sequins. The yoke
is of satin (*atlas*), edged with
zigzag appliqué (*tishrimeh*), with
a patch of luxury velvet.
135 × 94 cm (53 × 37 in)

THE BEADED AND TASSELLED TIES CLOSING THE SKIRT AND NECK OPENINGS WERE SUPPOSED
TO ATTRACT MALE ATTENTION. BLUE BEADS WERE ALSO BELIEVED TO AVERT THE EVIL EYE.

DRESS (*THOB*)
Deir Terif, near Jaffa, 1930s–1940s

The ribbed silk fabric (*kermesot*) is decorated with couching in silk cord and metallic threads filled with satin stitch. The techniques and patterns originated in Bethlehem, but have a unique character all of their own.
139 × 138 cm (54 3/4 × 54 1/2 in)

THE SIMPLE FLORAL MOTIFS ON THE BACK OF THE SKIRT (RIGHT) ARE PARTICULARLY STRIKING AGAINST THE PURPLE BACKGROUND.

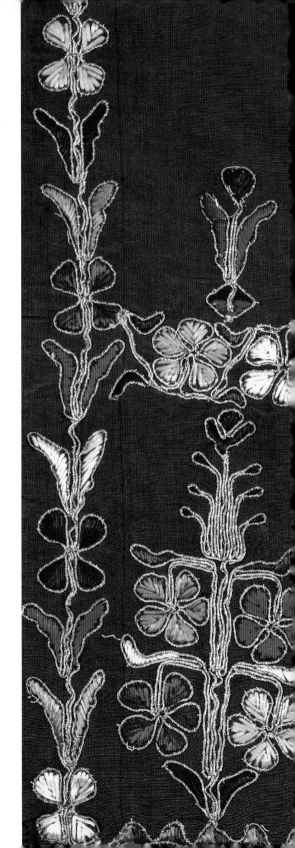

DRESS (*THOB*)
al-Na'ani, south of Ramleh, 1930s–1940s

The fabric is blue-black linen. It is decorated
with mainly cross-stitch embroidery, simple couching in
white cord on the yoke and satin-stitch seam stitching. This
village was famous for its fine cross stitch, which was
emulated by neighbouring villages. The embroidery is
particularly dense on the chest square (left). The bird (below)
and other motifs (right) show European influence.
140 × 150 cm (55 × 59 in)

THE NECK TIES, WITH THEIR IMITATION
PEARLS, BLUE BEADS AND SILK
TASSELS, PROVIDE AN EYE-CATCHING
CONTRAST TO THE GENERALLY
RESTRAINED DECORATION OF THE REST
OF THIS DRESS.

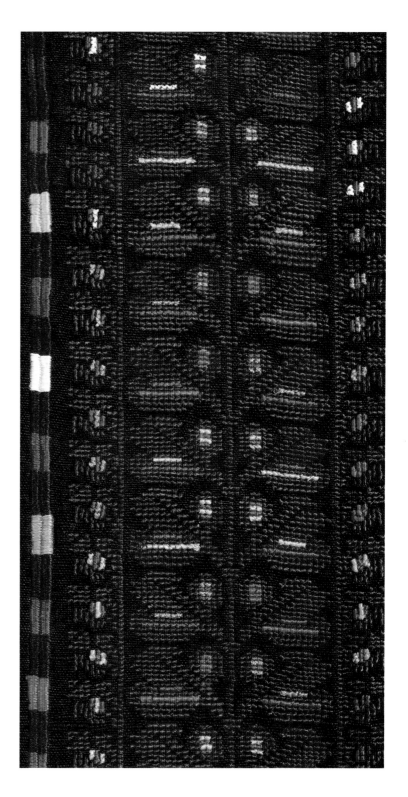

DRESS (*THOB*)
South-west coastal plain, *c.* 1920s

This indigo-blue cotton dress has cross-stitch embroidery in shades of red, orange and mauve with touches of other colours. The sides have been salvaged from an older garment. The chest square and sleeves probably date from the 1930s or 1940s.
140 × 133 cm (55 × 52$\frac{1}{2}$ in)

THE HARMONY OF WARM COLOURS MAKES THE SIMPLE GEOMETRIC PATTERNS MORE INTERESTING AND BEAUTIFUL.

DRESS (*THOB*)
Bethlehem area, probably
late 19th century

The 'royal' (*malak*) fabric of striped silk
and linen was woven locally. The yoke is of
European cotton. There are yellow and red
taffeta (*heremzi*) inserts in the sleeves and
skirt sides. The chest panel is of red, green
and yellow taffeta appliqué with zigzag
(*tishrimeh*) edges, surmounted
by strips of metallic brocade.
168 × 83 cm (66 × 32¹/₂ in)

THIS DRESS COMBINES SEVERAL LUXURY
FABRICS OF VARIOUS ORIGINS. ITS MOST
STRIKING FEATURE IS THE CHEST PANEL,
WITH ITS CONTRASTING COLOURS AND
ZIGZAG EDGES.

DRESS (*THOB IKHDARI*)
Bethlehem area, late 19th century

The main fabric is linen with
silk selvedge stripes. There are red and yellow
taffeta inserts in the sleeves and skirt. The
chest panel is couched with gilt cord and
yellow and green silk cord, and filled with
multicoloured satin and herringbone stitches.
The green and red taffeta background panel
can be glimpsed between the motifs, and the
panel has a yellow taffeta zigzag edging.
151 × 140 cm (39$^{1}/_{2}$ × 55 in)

THE FLOWING CURVILINEAR PATTERNS WITHIN
RECTANGULAR FRAMES, WARM HARMONIOUS
COLOURS AND LUSTROUS SILKS MAKE THIS
ONE OF THE MOST BEAUTIFUL EXAMPLES OF
BETHLEHEM EMBROIDERY.

125

JACKET (*TAQSIREH*)
Bethlehem area, 19th or
early 20th century

The dark blue velvet is embroidered
with gilt-cord couching filled with
satin stitch. The simple wreath
pattern is also found on the side
and sleeve panels of *malak* dresses
from the same period.
48 × 78 cm (19 × 30³/4 in)
Donated by Jerusalem and
the East Mission

VELVET ONLY BECAME WIDESPREAD FROM THE 1930s, SO WAS A GREAT LUXURY AT THIS EARLY PERIOD. IT PROVIDES A PERFECT BACKGROUND FOR THE LUXURIOUS YET RESTRAINED COUCHING.

DRESS (*THOB MALAK*)
Bethlehem area, late 19th or early 20th century

The dress takes its name (which means 'royal
dress') from the expensive striped linen and silk
fabric which was woven locally. The taffeta
(*heremzi*) panels inserted and applied on the
sleeves, side skirt panels and chest square are
couched in silk and metallic cord filled with satin,
herringbone and satin stitches in floss silk.
133 × 146 cm (52¹/₂ × 57¹/₂ in)
Donated by Jerusalem and
the East Mission

THIS DRESS COMBINES SEVERAL LUXURY
FABRICS OF VARIOUS ORIGINS. ITS MOST
STRIKING FEATURE IS THE CHEST PANEL, WITH
ITS CONTRASTING COLOURS AND ZIGZAG
EDGES. IT IS STRUCTURED IN THE SAME WAY AS
THAT ILLUSTRATED ON PAGES 124-5, BUT THE
EMBROIDERY IS DENSER AND MORE INTRICATE.

LEFT: DELICATE CROSS-STITCH
MOTIFS ON A TAFFETA SKIRT PANEL
OF THE BETHLEHEM 'ROYAL DRESS'
ILLUSTRATED ON THE PREVIOUS
PAGES.

RIGHT: COUCHING IN SILK AND
METALLIC CORD ON THE TAFFETA
SLEEVE PANELS OF THE SAME
DRESS.

THE TAFFETA PANELS ARE JOINED
BY A FORM OF HERRINGBONE
STITCH IN MANY COLOURS. THE
WREATH MOTIF IS SURMOUNTED
BY A TYPICAL BETHLEHEM BIRD.

VEIL (*KHIRQAH*)
Bethlehem, 19th century

The cotton veil is embroidered along four sides in stem stitch and broken running stitch. It has a matching multicoloured fringe.
235 × 95 cm (92 1/2 × 37 1/2 in)

THE DELICATE SHADES AND PATTERNS OF THIS FINE VEIL ARE REMINISCENT OF GREEK ISLAND EMBROIDERY.

chapter 3

Embroidery from Afghanistan

Detail from a panel (*ilgitsh*) intended to hang as a work of art. Red fulled wool worked in a range of stitches and in a variety of pastel-coloured silks. The motifs, which include scorpians, echo the shamanistic past of the Lakai tribe of ethnic Uzbeks. Northern Afghanistan, 19th or early 20th century. 64 x 64 cm (25 x 25 $^1/_2$ in).

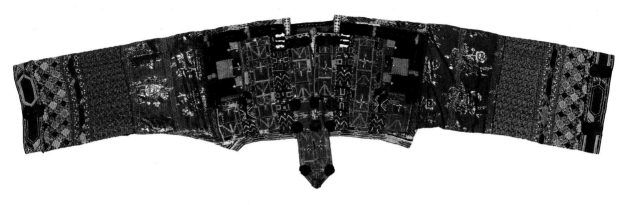

WOMAN'S DRESS BODICE
The Kakarh (Pashtun) people

The Kakarh are a mountain people, clinging to ancient beliefs. They remove the skirt of a dress before selling it, considering it too intimate for others to own. It is, in any case, generally plain and also heavy to carry to market.

Pieced from several older embroideries, the dress top combines areas of dense stitchery with others of fabric, such as satin and gold brocade. Patterns are geometric or stylized floral; black pompoms punctuate the bodice front.
38 × 145 cm (15 × 57 in)

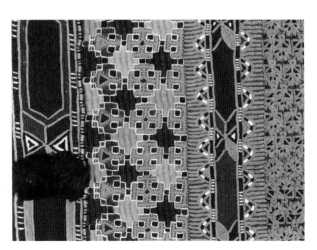

THE HOTCHPOTCH OF PIECED EMBROIDERIES IN A FAIRLY LIMITED COLOUR RANGE GIVES THIS DRESS AN EXUBERANT VIBRANCY, ACCENTUATED BY THE SPACE-DEFINING AREAS OF BLACK.

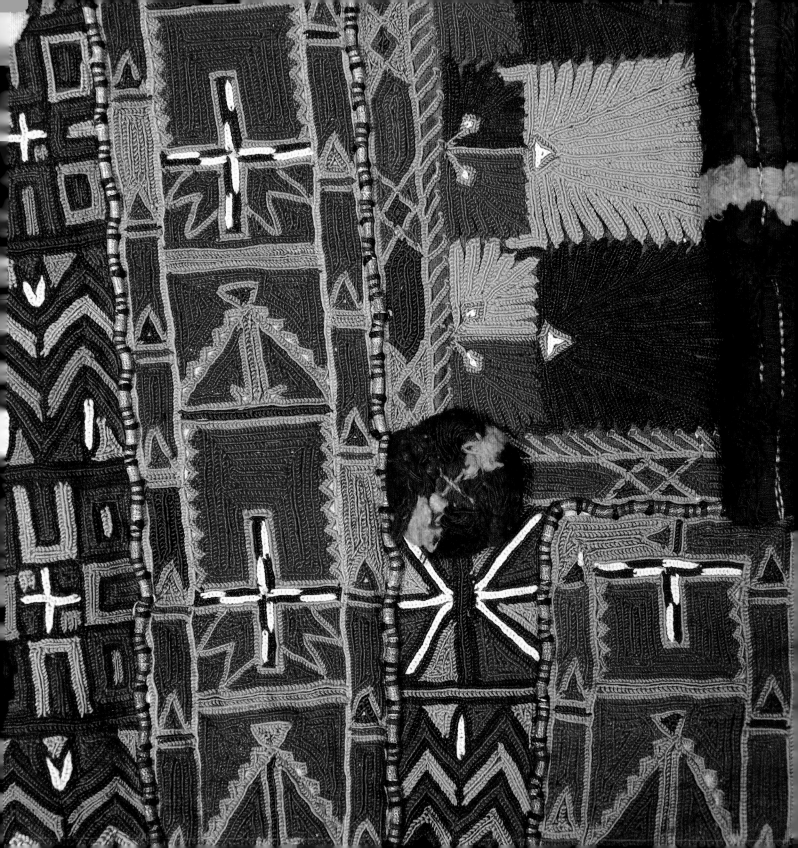

WOMAN'S DRESS
The Koochi, eastern and southern Afghanistan

The Koochi are nomadic herders and gypsies and their clothing is
particularly flamboyant. Their dresses, brought back to the West, are
those that identified Afghanistan in the 1970s hippie era.

This dress is of floral print velvet. The back, which would be covered with
a shawl, is in cotton. The embroidery includes fine interlacing
in yellow. The bodice is heavily covered with coins and
beadwork, including *gul-i-peron* discs; while these have an
ancient history, the silver cording on the hem is modern.
120 × 35 cm (47 × 14 in)

THE OVERLOAD OF MATERIALS, PATTERNS, BEADS AND
COINS SHOULD NOT BE PLEASING, BUT IT DOES CREATE
A DENSITY THAT IS NON-CONFRONTATIONAL.

FESTIVE TABLECLOTH
Tajik people, northern Afghanistan, *c.*1940

This tablecloth is made from three pieces of purple
silk cloth, which is produced in Kabul, Herat and Multan. The
stylized depiction of a peacock is very unusual in Afghan embroideries,
though similar birds and animals are sometimes found on Uzbek *suzanis*.

Flower heads and buds like pomegranates are the other motifs, worked in Bukhara
couching in heavy floss silk in vivid colours. Pomegranates are a common
symbol of fertility, so the cloth was probably created for marriage.
96 × 64 cm (38 × 25 in)

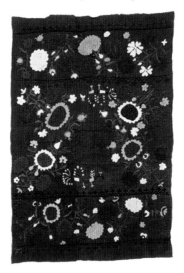

THE PLAIN CENTRE EMPHASIZES THE STRONG
REVOLVING ASPECT OF THE BRIGHT MOTIFS
AROUND IT, WHILE THE BIRD ACTS AS A FOCUS.

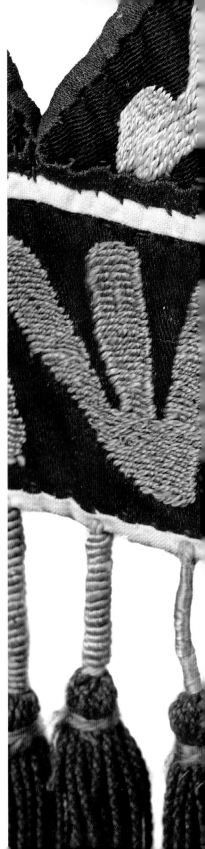

HORSE HEADCOVER
Uzbek people, northern Afghanistan

Decorative animal trappings, especially for horses
and camels, are used for special occasions such as marriage or
even market days. They emphasize the importance of domesticated
animals in the steppe economy.

This cover for a horse's head is made of black- and cinnamon-coloured
cotton, lined with oddments of floral and geometric printed cotton. The
horned and branch-like motifs are embroidered in Bukhara couching.
The cover is edged with tassels on wrapped cords, ending in small white
beads, which is typical of much of the embroidery of Central Asia.
53 × 52 cm (21 × 20½ in)

THIS REGAL HEADCOVER ALMOST HAS THE ASPECT OF A CROWN,
IN SPITE OF ITS SIMPLE MATERIALS, STITCHERY AND DESIGN.

SMALL HANGING FOR A YURT
Uzbek people, northern Afghanistan, 1960–70

Decorative hangings were usually put up near
the entrance of the yurt; they could also be placed
between piled-up quilts.

The lower part of this Uzbek hanging is solid embroidery in cross
stitch with hooked motifs. These motifs, their colours and repetition,
are common in the embroideries of Tajikistan and Sukhandaria in
southern Uzbekistan. The top part is a print fabric, probably
from Ivanovo. This town, north-east of Moscow, was an
important source of the printed cottons used throughout Central
Asia as linings. The embroidery ends in tassels on wrapped cords.
64 × 11 cm (25 × 4½ in)

THE INTEREST IN THIS SMALL PIECE DERIVES FROM THE CONTRAST
BETWEEN THE PRINTED TOP PART AND THE EMBROIDERED LOWER
SECTION, CUT OFF IN MID-PATTERN.

PANEL (*ILGITSH*)
Lakai Uzbek, northern Afghanistan

Many Lakai embroideries are non-functional panels for
the walls of the yurt, placed on opposite sides of the bedding pile.
As this piece is fringed all round, it was probably a cover for food.

It is made of red fulled wool, which was usually traded into
Uzbekistan from Russia. The design is based on a horned square,
centred by a four-leaved square. The stitches are fine slanting
blanket, mainly in yellow, green and blue. The two anthropomorphic
figures in the navy cotton border are highly unusual.
39 × 37 cm (15¹/₂ × 14¹/₂ in)

THIS PIECE INTRODUCES US TO THE DISTINCTIVE CHARACTERISTICS
OF LAKAI WORK – VIBRANT MOVEMENT, POWERFUL ABSTRACT
DESIGN AND CLEARLY DEFINED EMBROIDERY.

MARRIAGE CANOPY
Lakai Uzbek, northern Afghanistan

Most embroideries were made by the bride, as in Uzbekistan,
in the months or weeks she was kept in seclusion in preparation for marriage.

Red fulled wool has been worked in slanting blanket stitch in fine multicoloured silks.
The cross-stitch border closely resembles the work of Tajikistan and southern Uzbekistan.
It is edged by a *djiyak* band and a netting of repeated colours, with
tassels held by metal grips.
173 × 158 cm (68 × 62 in)

THE SYMBOLISM OF MARRIAGE IS
WELL PORTRAYED IN THE TWO
BIRDS, WHICH SEEM PROTECTIVELY
ENCLOSED BY THE EMBROIDERY
AND THE DECORATIVE NETTING.

149

PANEL (*ILGITSH*)
Lakai Uzbek, northern Afghanistan

Much embroidery of Lakai women is talismanic, holding
the power to protect the yurt and the family. Its symbolism, however, is often
confused and complex. This is another non-functional decoration.

The red fulled wool is embroidered in a range of vivid colours in slanting
blanket and chain stitch. Some motifs could be insects, others pomegranates,
while the stars and triangles are rounded and softened.
57 × 59 cm (22^1/$_2$ × 23^1/$_2$ in)

THOUGH THE MOTIFS ARE BALANCED ON THE BACKGROUND, THE
VARIETY WITHIN THEM LEADS TO A DENSE DESIGN WHICH IS BUSY
BUT NOT OVERCROWDED.

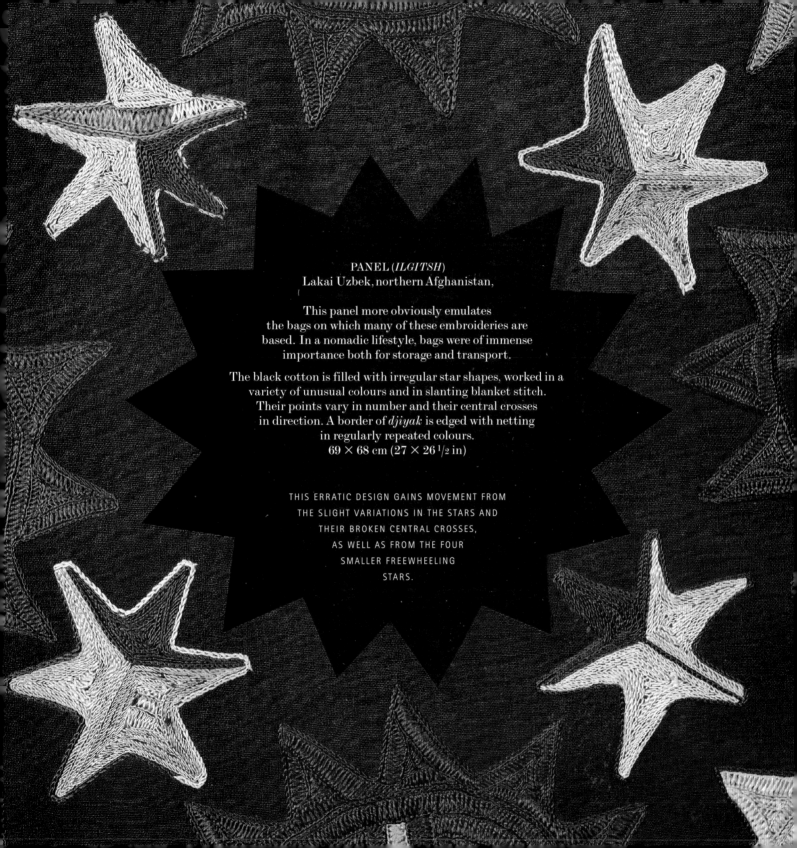

PANEL (*ILGITSH*)
Lakai Uzbek, northern Afghanistan,

This panel more obviously emulates
the bags on which many of these embroideries are
based. In a nomadic lifestyle, bags were of immense
importance both for storage and transport.

The black cotton is filled with irregular star shapes, worked in a
variety of unusual colours and in slanting blanket stitch.
Their points vary in number and their central crosses
in direction. A border of *djiyak* is edged with netting
in regularly repeated colours.
69 × 68 cm (27 × 26 1/2 in)

THIS ERRATIC DESIGN GAINS MOVEMENT FROM
THE SLIGHT VARIATIONS IN THE STARS AND
THEIR BROKEN CENTRAL CROSSES,
AS WELL AS FROM THE FOUR
SMALLER FREEWHEELING
STARS.

SYMBOLIC BAG (*BOTCHA*)
Lakai Uzbek, northern Afghanistan

This bag, which is actually a flat panel with a flap,
derives its shape from ancient 'envelope' bags. Some
examples can merely have the flap suggested by stitching.

The black fulled wool is embroidered in *kesdi* and chain in sombre
colours that are also used in the fringe. Six circles are worked with
slight differences in colour and placing, though the ones at the top,
lower centre and side are essentially the same. Different colour
balance transforms the motifs, giving an appearance of asymmetry.
64 × 60 cm (25 × 23 1/2 in)

THE WHOLE DESIGN IS SET IN MOTION BY THE VARIATION IN THE MOTIFS AT
LOWER LEFT AND RIGHT, AND THE SLIGHTLY OFF-CENTRE ORANGE PATCH.

HORSE
HEADCOVER
Lakai Uzbek, northern
Afghanistan

The Lakai ethos was based on horsemanship –
first as horse-thieves, then as breeders. Both men
and women rode and regalia for horses was an
important element of their textiles. Similar
headcovers were made for camels.

This example, of red fulled wool, is embroidered in Bukhara couching.
The hanging padded rolls end in goat-hair tufts. The lining is an old block-
printed fabric, probably from Khiva in northern Uzbekistan.
95 × 40 cm (37$^1/_2$ × 16 in)

THE STRENGTH OF THE DESIGN LIES IN THE ESOTERIC
COLOURS AND THE ERRATIC DEPICTION OF WHAT
MIGHT NORMALLY BE PRECISE GEOMETRIC
MOTIFS, SOME FACING TOWARDS
EACH OTHER AND SOME
AWAY.

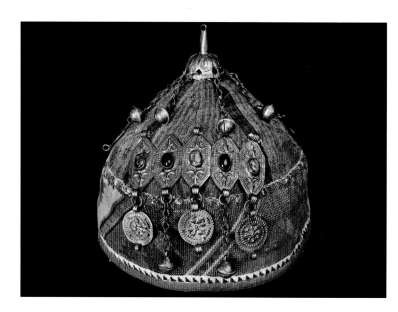

GIRL'S CAP

Turkmen people, northern Afghanistan

Such caps, with a silver finial and rows of silver links, are worn by girls of marriageable age. The embossed silver work is characteristic of the Yomut tribe, while the more famous Tekke work is plain and dramatic, enhanced by cornelian stones.

The base of the cap is completely covered with geometric patterns in cross stitch, while the crown is in couching. The embossed metal discs and links with glass beads are typical of the Turkmen. Bells are considered amuletic.

BECAUSE OF THE TIGHT, BUT RATHER RANDOM, PATTERN AND THE COLOURING OF THE EMBROIDERY, THE SILVER BELLS AND AMULETS MERGE INTO THE DESIGN.

WOMAN'S CLOAK (*CHYRPY*)
Tekke Turkmen, Turkmenistan and northern Afghanistan, early 20th century

These densely embroidered cloaks were worn throughout Tekke Turkmen territory,
and still are for marriage, while plainer versions are for every day.

The cloak is worn over the head with the vestigial sleeves hanging down the back. This
dark green fabric is for a young girl, while yellow is for a married woman and white for
an elderly woman. The main motif is the tulip: a symbol of fertility as it is the first
flower to bloom on the steppes in spring. The stitch is *kesdi*.
102 × 65 cm (40 × 25 1/2 in)

CHYRPYS ALWAYS HAVE A BORDER OF MUCH FINER EMBROIDERY ROUND
THE NECK, AND CONTRASTING ENDS TO THE 'SLEEVES'. THESE ADD AN
ELEMENT OF CONTRAST TO THE ALL-OVER PATTERNING.

WOMAN'S DRESS
Baluch people, southern Afghanistan

A defining feature of Baluchi dresses is the front pocket from waist to hem (*pudo*). The women often keep money or keys in it, though it can be merely decorative.

The vivid pink wool of this dress is exquisitely embroidered, mainly in the yellow interlacing stitch in vertical bands, which is typical of the Baluch. The motifs are focused by a few pieces of *shisha* mirror. Breast slits are outlined in blue fabric and have appliquéd triangles as amulets. The embroidery round the neck represents a necklace that the woman would no doubt have been unable to afford.

THE STRONG COLOUR OF THIS DRESS IS OFFSET BY THE DELICATE WORKMANSHIP AND COLOUR OF THE INTERLACING STITCH. A STRIKING FEATURE IS THE TWO SLITS TO FACILITATE BREAST-FEEDING.

PURSE COVER
Hazara people, Oruzgan

Small rectangular purses were made by the Hazara
to hold precious objects, including soil brought by
pilgrims from the holy Shia site of Kerbela.

The fabric is fine cotton, solidly worked in brick
stitch in silk, the colours alternating green and
orange, pink and purple. Diamond motifs surround
hooked diamonds. These Hazara stitches
and patterns were chosen by the DACAAR
scheme (see p. 25) to support Afghan refugees
because of their appeal to European taste.
30 × 12 cm (12 × 4³/₄ in)

THIS DESIGN COULD APPEAR
STATIC AND RIGID, BUT THE
CHOICE OF A VERY LIMITED
RANGE OF COLOURS GIVES IT
A COOL ELEGANCE.

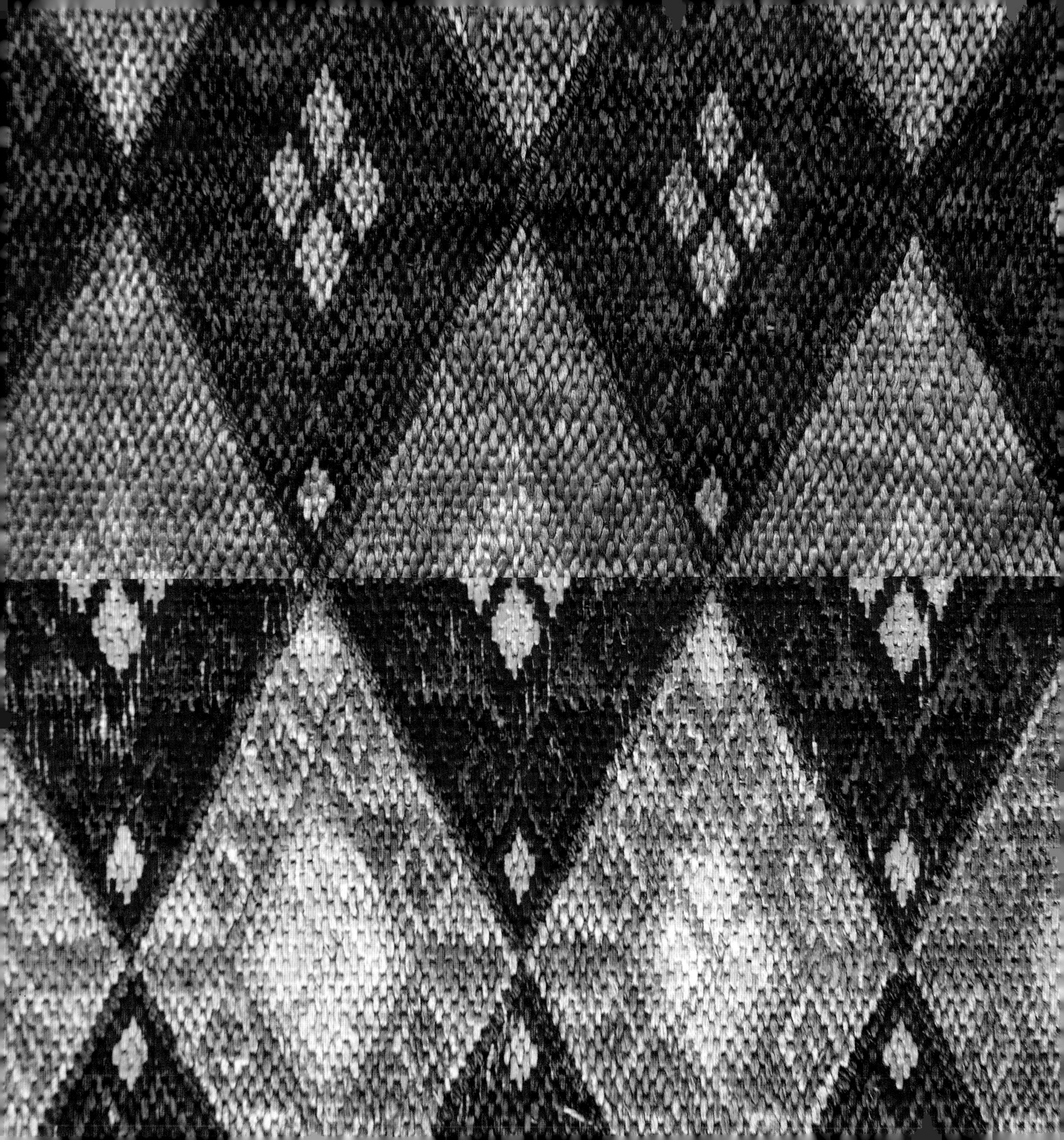

PURSE
Hazara people, Oruzgan

Such envelope-shaped purses are used to hold treasures,
smaller versions being made for *kohl*. They are usually closed by wrapping
thread round them. The two small tassels would hold this thread.

A square of fine cotton, with visible weave suitable for the counted-thread
technique, is worked solidly in brick stitch in various colours of silk.
The edging is overstitched in alternating green and brown.
15 × 9 cm (6 × 3 1/2 in)

FOLDING THE PURSE INTO AN ENVELOPE, AS IT WAS INTENDED TO
BE USED, CREATES A VIBRANT ZIGZAG PATTERN, ACCENTUATED BY
THE SINGLE BLACK LINE.

chapter 4

Embroidery from India and Pakistan

Detail from a woman's backless blouse (*choli*) made of lightweight silk fabric embroidered in very fine chain stitch in the style of the Mochi. The drawn design is unworked in some places and still visible. Lohana community, Kutch, north-west India, 20th century. 32 x 84 cm ($12^1/_2$ x 33 in).

DOOR HANGING (*TORAN*)
Mehr farmers, Saurashtra, north-west India, 20th century

These embroideries are hung above doorways on special occasions, or over shrines.
They are often complemented by side hangings, *sakhyo*.

Made of white cotton, this *toran* is embroidered in silk threads in herringbone stitch outlined
with chain stitch. The flower motifs are centred with *shisha* and the borders are of appliquéd
cotton strips. The main motif is of blue-faced Krishna playing the flute. He is accompanied by
the sacred cow, symbol of the Mother Earth, which is often associated with him.
66 × 128 cm (26 × 50⅓ in)

THE VIVACIOUS MOTIFS OF HINDU SYMBOLISM ARE BALANCED BY THE FINE
GEOMETRY OF THE PENDANTS AND THE RESTRAINED SYMMETRY OF THE FLORAL
AND LEAF BORDER. THE LIVELY, BALANCED PALETTE OF RED, PURPLE, FUCHSIA,
GREEN AND YELLOW IS USED TO GREAT EFFECT.

THE FORMALITY OF THE
BASIC DIAMOND DESIGN IS
GIVEN ADDED INTEREST BY
THE INTRODUCTION OF A
TRIANGULAR PATTERN AT
THE BOTTOM AND ALONG
ONE OF THE SIDES.

NECKPIECE (*GALLA*)
Banjara community, Deccan, central India

Neckpieces of this kind hang over the back of a woman's head, protecting her
nape from the strong sun. They are usually attached to a padded ring on her
head, called an *indohni*, which enables her to carry heavy water-pots.

The cinnamon-coloured cotton is solidly embroidered in brick stitch, in
cotton thread. The edging of cowrie shells is traditional, and matted
pompoms of purple silk give added talismanic protection.
36 × 23 cm (14 × 9 in), including tassels and cowries.

HAT
Possibly Himachal Pradesh, northern India

A most unusual cotton fabric hat with a deep crown
and rising flaps at the side, which are padded with wool
and edged with large tassels. The embroidery is entirely
in chain stitch, with circles of colour on the crown and
black-and-white diamond shapes at the front and
on the flaps. A cord loops under the chin.
27 × 15.5 cm (10$^1/_2$ × 6 in) excluding tassels
Donated by Mrs P. Lambert

A WONDERFUL EXAMPLE OF TEXTURE — THE SMOOTH
EFFECT OF THE CIRCLES ON THE CROWN AND THE
VERY ROUGH TASSELS AROUND IT ARE PULLED
TOGETHER VISUALLY BY THE USE OF COLOUR.

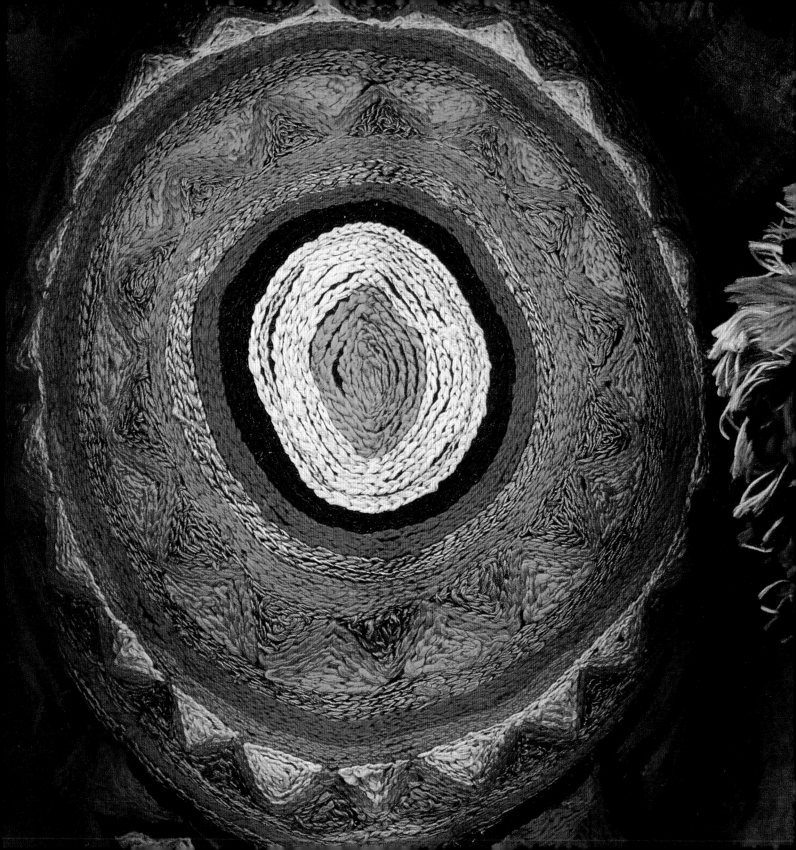

THE MARRIAGE CANOPY (*CHANDARVO*)
Patel farmers, Saurashtra, north-west India

These canopies are erected outside the bride's home on the
occasion of a marriage, and sometimes even hung across the street.

The base fabric is plain white cotton, embroidered in multicoloured cotton thread, mainly
in herringbone stitch. The pattern features various Hindu deities, including Ganesh the
elephant god, remover of obstacles and a favourite motif in household textiles.
180 cm (71 in) square

THIS PATTERN IS DIVIDED INTO FOUR SECTIONS REVOLVING AROUND A CENTRAL ROSETTE, WITH NO TOP OR BOTTOM. VIEWING IT FROM BELOW, THERE IS ENDLESS DETAIL TO BE ABSORBED. THE MOTIFS ARE HEAVY WITH SYMBOLISM.

FOR THE COUPLE, THE PEACOCK BRINGS FERTILITY AND HAPPINESS, AND BOTH THE ELEPHANT (LEFT) AND THE HORSE (PICTURED ON PAGE 29) DENOTE PROSPERITY. THE ELEPHANT IS ASSOCIATED WITH LAKSHMI, GODDESS OF WEALTH.

BAG
Banjara community, Deccan, central India

Bags were used for many purposes by these semi-
nomadic people, and were usually envelope-shaped.

The fabric is a heavy natural cotton, solidly worked in
wool threads, mainly in brick stitch. The corners and
sides of the flaps are decorated with small wool
pompoms and cowries on fabric rouleaux.
42 × 41 cm (16^{1}/$_{2}$ × 16 in)

THIS BAG HAS AN
UNUSUALLY LOVELY
COLOUR RANGE,
THE INTRODUCTION
OF GREEN ADDING
TO THE DEPTH OF
COLOUR ACHIEVED.

THE COWRIE SHELL
IS BELIEVED TO
HAVE PROTECTIVE
POWERS AND SO
FEATURES ON ITEMS
HOLDING PRECIOUS
OBJECTS.

WEDDING MAT (*RUMAL*)
Banjara community, Deccan, central India

A small mat used to cover food at
marriage ceremonies.

The mat is made of a square of natural-coloured cotton
appliquéd with patches of indigo- and brick-coloured
cotton, and with finer white cotton cut in a zigzag line.
The embroidery is mainly chain stitch in wool
thread, with some touches of fine white cotton. The
four larger central squares are highlighted with *shisha*.
65 cm (25$\frac{1}{2}$ in) square

A PAINTERLY VIBRANCY IS
ACHIEVED THROUGH DEPTH OF
COLOUR ON A LIGHT GROUND.

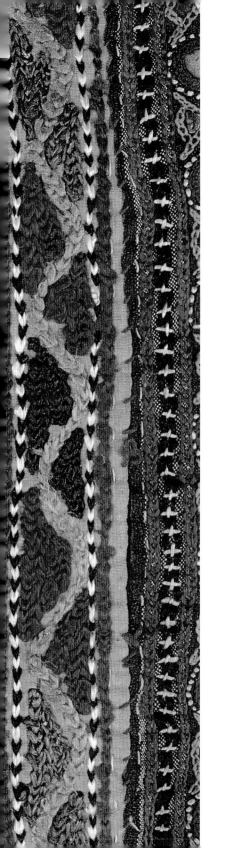

WOMAN'S BACKLESS BLOUSE (*CHOLI*)
Possibly Kutch, north-west India

This blouse is unusual in shape, in that the plain
central band gathers up to fit around the breasts, with
ties that end in tassels and cardamom seeds.

Pieces of fine silk are patched together
to form the blouse. The sides and bodice top are
entirely covered in *shisha* in a six-petalled floral motif,
enhanced by red silk pompoms. The embroidery
is in silk thread, mainly in chain stitch.
67 cm (26 in) × 75 cm (29 1/2 in) across arms

THE SKIRT'S CENTRAL PANEL WITH ITS SIMPLE
MOTIFS AND BRIGHT YELLOW COLOUR STANDS OUT,
INTRODUCING VITALITY TO THE WHOLE DESIGN.

A LIVELY FEELING OF MOVEMENT IS ACHIEVED BY THE ASYMMETRICAL PATTERNING AND THE ADDITION OF TASSELS APPLIED IN A CIRCULAR DIRECTION.

NUT HOLDER
Banjara community, Deccan, central India

This holder, like the bags of the Banjara, is particularly suited to a nomadic way of life. Nuts and other precious articles can be stored and hung in safety.

The holder is made of four square bags of cinnamon-coloured cotton cloth and one central square. The hanging bags are solidly embroidered on both sides in cotton thread, mainly in brick stitch, with some cross stitch. The rouleau tassels end in wool pompoms.
57 cm (22 in) square

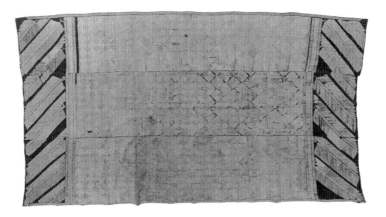

WOMAN'S SHAWL (*BAGH*)
West Punjab, Pakistan

These shawls were begun by the grandmother at the time
of a child's birth. If a girl, she would wear it at her marriage.
If a boy, it would drape his bride. In the *phulkari* tradition,
when these shawls are almost completely covered with
stitchery they are known as a *bagh* (garden).

Loosely woven, cinnamon-coloured cotton (*khaddar*) is
worked in surface darning stitch from the back. The thread is
yellow floss silk, and normally a small touch of contrast is
added — in this case, a patch of deep brownish-red.
245 × 133 cm (96½ × 52 in). Donated by Lady Menendez

THIS SHAWL, WITH ITS RESTRAINED DUOTONE, DEPENDS ENTIRELY
FOR ITS EFFECT ON THE PLAY OF LIGHT PERMEATING THE DESIGN
WITH AN AUSTERE BEAUTY.

WOMAN'S DRESS (*PASHK*)
Baluchistan, southern Pakistan, *c.*1920

A woman's dress of the Baluchi people from near the Afghan border. The bodice front is densely embroidered, as is the *pudo*, a pocket extending from the hem to an upward-pointing triangle over the genital area.

The dress is constructed of rectangles of fabric, with shaped sleeves and a contrasting underarm gusset of brocaded silk. The linear division of the embroidery, using rows of chain stitch and black threads couched in white, extends into a wider band of patterning over the breast. The hem and seams are worked in red interlacing and orange herringbone.
108 cm (42$\frac{1}{2}$ in) × 146 cm (57$\frac{1}{2}$ in) across arms.
Donated by Mrs Doreen Ellis

THE RICHLY BOLD PALETTE OF BALUCHI EMBROIDERY IS USED HERE AGAINST A GROUND OF PURPLE SILK. AN EXCITING EFFECT IS CREATED BY THE STRICT DIVISION OF THE DESIGN INTO CONTRASTING AREAS OF DENSELY WORKED EMBROIDERY AND PLAIN FABRIC, TYPICAL OF BALUCHI WORK.

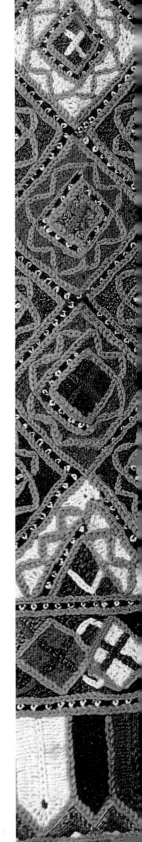

CHILD'S JACKET (*KERIYA*)
Lohana community, Sindh, southern Pakistan

Beautiful jackets such as this were commonly worn by small
children throughout north-west India and Sindh.

The motifs on this jacket, which is made of orange silk, are
embroidered mainly in buttonhole stitch and radiating stitch,
in silk threads. The borders and dividing lines are edged with
commercial ricrac and accentuated with sequins. There is one
central *shisha* on the front and two on the back: one at the nape
and the other at the waist.
52 cm (20¹/₂ in) × 56.5 cm (22¹/₄ in) across arms

THE DESIGN IS AT ONCE FORMAL AND FREE-FLOWING, ALLOWING THE PRACTICALITIES OF THE
DRESS SHAPE TO INFLUENCE THE PATTERNING.

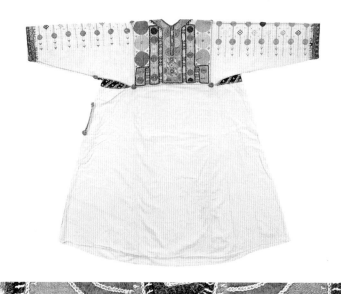

WOMAN'S DRESS
Sindh, southern Pakistan

Long dresses of this type were worn in Sindh and by the Bugti and Brahui of Baluchistan. The contrasting underarm gusset is typical of the region right through to Afghanistan.

This dress of white cotton is very finely embroidered in silk threads of pastel colours, in radiating stitch with some chain and herringbone. Pink silk fabric, flanked by yellow, is appliquéd at the neck and outlined with a row of black threads couched in white. Circular patterns in radiating stitch are a feature of Sindhi embroidery.

112 cm (44 in) × 134 cm (52³/₄ in) across arms

LIMITING THE PALETTE TO SOFT PINKS AND YELLOWS AND THE DESIGN TO ALMOST

ENTIRELY CIRCULAR SHAPES IMBUES THIS EMBROIDERY WITH A DELICATE SUBTLETY.

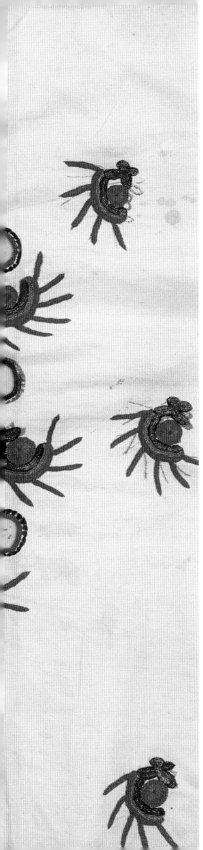

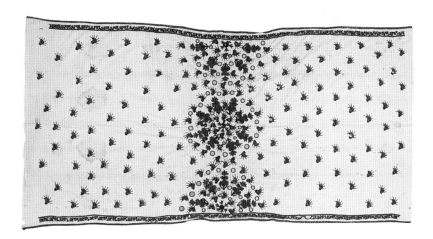

WOMAN'S WEDDING SHAWL (*ABOCHHINI*)
Tharparkar, southern Pakistan

Such shawls are common throughout the region of
the Tharparkar desert and the Indus delta.

Made of white cotton, this shawl is embroidered in
red and green silk with floral motifs in radiating
and open chain stitch. Large pieces of *shisha*
decorate the central band, across which are three
pompoms with cardamom seeds.
135 × 255 cm (53 × 100 in)

VERY SIMPLE COLOURING IS USED IN THIS DESIGN WHICH IS BUILT UP USING
ONLY THREE BASIC MOTIFS. ITS IMPACT IS ACHIEVED BY MULTIPLYING THESE
MOTIFS INTO THREE DENSE AREAS OF PATTERN IN THE CENTRE.

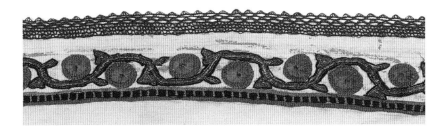

chapter 5

Miao Textiles from China

Decorative detail from a woman's festive jacket made from cotton and satin. The decorative area shown consists of starched silk rectangles, folded into triangles and stitched through the points. Tiny, intricate geometric shapes, bordered by linear braids or ribbons, are built up to form a variety of gem-like motifs, no two of which are the same. The colour is predominantly azure blue with flashes of white, purple and orange. Taijiang County, Qiandongnan Prefecture, 20th century. 93 x 109 cm ($36^1/_2$ x 43 in).

FEMALE FESTIVE COSTUME
Weining County, Bijie Prefecture, 1920s

The short collared jacket with wide sleeves and attached cape is made of
two narrow widths of hemp cloth, seamed at the back and sides. Two
decorative woven rectangles joined at the centre back form the cape. The
sleeves are simple woven rectangles, attached to the underlayer. The
supplementary wool patterning is woven on a hemp ground and further
decorated with applied cloth.
55 cm × 175 cm (21³/₄ × 69 in)

THE JACKET BACK HAS A STRONG GEOMETRIC DESIGN PICKED OUT IN WHITE CLOTH, EDGED WITH RED. ON THE SHOULDERS IS A ZIGZAG

DESIGN IN RED AND BLACK. THE SLEEVE ECHOES THIS PATTERNING, BUT EMPLOYS ASYMMETRY TO CREATE ADDED INTEREST.

FEMALE EVERYDAY/FESTIVE JACKET
Nankai township, Liupanshui Prefecture,
20th century

Sleeveless cape with collar, tacked to a
collarless underlayer of hemp or ramie.

The decoration is made up of strips of
yellow, red, black, white and blue appliquéd
cotton strips, which surround rectangles and
squares embroidered in white, red and
green cross-stitch motifs.
66 × 73 cm (26 × 28³/₄ in)

THE DECEPTIVELY COMPLICATED DESIGN
EMPLOYS EMBROIDERED PANELS, FRAMED
WITHIN STRIPED BORDERS. IT IS UNIFIED
BY THE REPETITION OF THE SAME RED AND
GREEN IN BOTH ELEMENTS.

FEMALE FESTIVE JACKET
Xingren County, Xingyi Prefecture, 20th century

Long-sleeved jacket in which the front extends to the right side and ties under
the arm. The sides are open and there are five added triangles at each side.

There is an inner lining of chemically dyed blue manufactured cotton.
The back and front yoke is shiny green damask-type weave. The sleeve is decorated in
applied bands of embroidery and cloth. The lower back and front have applied
embroidered pieces worked in satin stitch, edged round the yoke with bought ribbon.
The collar and facing strip is embroidered with silk in satin stitch over paper.
45 × 115 cm (17³/₄ × 45¹/₄ in)

THE STRENGTH OF THIS DESIGN LIES IN ITS DIVISION OF SEPARATE AREAS OF
PATTERN. THE DRAMATIC GREEN CENTRE PANEL IS SLASHED BY THE COLLAR AND A
FACING STRIP. BELOW: THE LOWER FRONT PANEL IS RICHLY DECORATED.

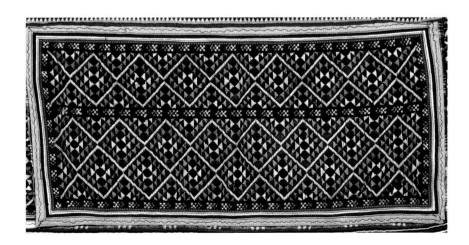

FEMALE FESTIVE JACKET
Near Anshun City, Anshun Prefecture, 20th century

Short, wide, long-sleeved collared jacket
with centre front opening.

It is decorated with applied rectangles of red
manufactured cotton embroidered with spiral
designs and circles, mainly in yellow
satin stitch and cross stitch.
60×172 cm ($23^{3}/_{4} \times 67^{3}/_{4}$ in)

THIS DESIGN, WITH PANELS EMBROIDERED IN PIERCINGLY BRIGHT COLOURS, IS
COUNTERBALANCED BY AREAS OF PLAIN FABRIC IN MATCHING COLOURS.

THIS DESIGN INTEGRATES
TWO TOTALLY DIFFERENT
CONTRASTING ELEMENTS.
THE LARGE SEMICIRCULAR
BACK PANEL AND SLEEVE
DETAIL FEATURES A RHYTHM
OF CIRCLES AND SPIRALS,
IN STARK CONTRAST TO
THE BRIGHTLY COLOURED
EMBROIDERED BIRDS AND
FLOWER DECORATIONS THAT
PUNCTUATE THE GARMENT.

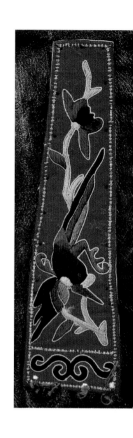

FEMALE FESTIVE JACKET
Duyun City area, Qiannan Prefecture, 20th century

Collared long-sleeved jacket, curved at the bottom edge
and fastened on the right side with a side opening.

The base cloth is hand-woven diamond twill, dyed indigo with a good
sheen on the outside. The upper sleeves and upper back panels are wax
resist. The silk satin epaulets, neck and front facings are embroidered in
satin stitch and outlined with a bound core thread couched on. Two small
red wool panels in the lower back are similarly embroidered.
75 × 134 cm (29^1/$_2$ × 52^3/$_4$ in)

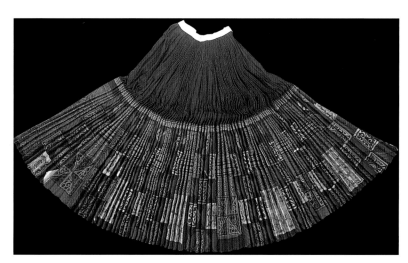

FEMALE SKIRT
Huishui County, Qiannan Prefecture,
20th century

Pleated skirt with 45 cm (17³/₄ in)
deep patchwork band.

The cloth of the lower section is hand-woven
cotton, dyed with indigo. It is stiffened and forms the
base of the patchwork. The upper part is manufactured
cotton dyed black with an undyed waistband. All the
complete squares are embroidered, some directly
on silk while others have cutaway cloth designs
outlined with couching threads.
79 × 80 cm (31 × 31¹/₂ in) at waist

THE IMPACT OF THIS DESIGN IS ACHIEVED BY
EMPLOYING A SIMPLE PATCHWORK IN WHICH
LARGER PANELS WORK AGAINST THE SMALLER
PATCHES TO CREATE A VIBRANT PATTERN. THE
FLASHES OF RED THROUGHOUT SET UP THE EFFECT
OF SYNCOPATED RHYTHM.

FEMALE FESTIVE JACKET
Danzhai County, Qiandongnan Prefecture, late 19th century
(according to Chinese sources)

A rare style, probably not worn today, this short collared jacket is slightly
flared at bottom, with wide sleeves and front opening.
The base lining is hand-woven unbleached cotton, the top layer a patchwork
of many different cloths. Both back and front have horizontal bands of
decoration which include embroidery and appliqué. The sleeves are banded
with appliqué, wax resist, shiny black cotton and pattern darning.
48.5 × 143.5 cm (19 × 56$^{1}/_{2}$ in)

THIS JACKET IS DECORATED WITH A COMBINATION OF BOLD GEOMETRIC PANELS CONTRASTING WITH AREAS OF INTRICATE WORK.

THE SLEEVE PANEL (LEFT), WORKED IN WAX RESIST, FEATURES EIGHT RADIATING SPIRALS ARRANGED IN A CIRCLE WITHIN A SQUARE.

'HUNDRED-BIRD COAT'
Rongjiang/Sandu County, Qiandongnan Prefecture,
*c.*1950–1990
Collarless jacket with open sides and sleeves and an attached 'skirt' of thirteen free-hanging panels. Worn at the Guzang festival held by the Miao at irregular intervals to renew and reinforce spiritual links with their ancestors. Probably worn by both men and women over their normal full costume.

The base cloth is undyed, hand-woven cotton. It is decorated with applied green sateen and embroidered with floss silk in satin stitch over papercuts in strong colours.
100 × 145cm (39¹/₂ × 57 in)

FESTIVAL JACKET
Danzhai County, Qiandongnan Prefecture,
20th century

As with the previous jacket, this collarless sleeved
jacket with attached 'skirt' of twelve hanging
panels was worn over a complete costume at
festivals, probably by men and women alike.

The base cloth is undyed hand-woven cotton in
diamond twill weave. On the decorated areas are
thin sheets of applied light green 'silk felt'
embroidered with satin-stitch motifs.
135 × 160 cm (53 × 63 in)

OPPOSITE: THE BACK PANEL FEATURES ROWS OF
PAIRED STYLIZED BIRDS SET IN A DIAMOND,
SURROUNDED BY LARGER, MORE ELABORATE BIRD
MOTIFS. THE MUTED COLOURS HARMONIZE THE
VARIOUS ELEMENTS OF THE DESIGN.

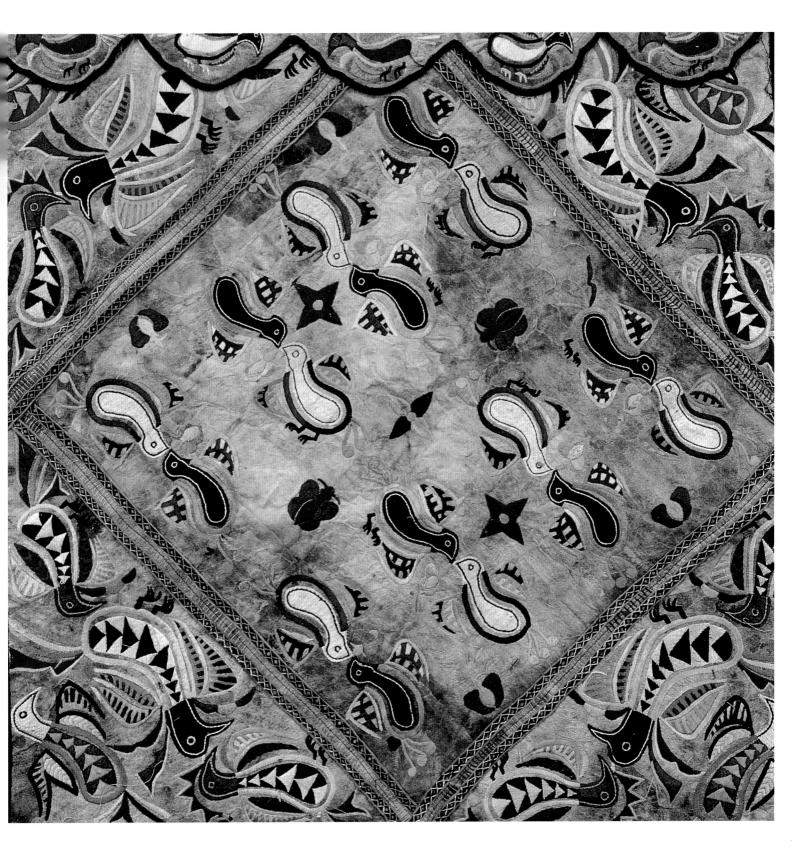

WOMAN'S FESTIVE JACKET
Taijiang County, Qiandongnan Prefecture, 20th century

Collared jacket with a central front opening, with decoration
on the sleeves, shoulders, neck and front facings.

The base cloth is hand-woven cotton, indigo-dyed to a dark blue. There is
no inner lining. The finely drawn and detailed decorative panels are
embroidered in floss silk in satin stitch over papercuts.
81 × 130 cm (32 × 51 1/4 in)

THE ZOOMORPHIC MOTIFS,
WITH STRONG ANTHROPO-
MORPHIC OVERTONES, ARE
WORKED IN SILVERY SOFT
PURPLE AND WATERY PALE

BLUE SILKS. THE PLEASING
SUBTLETY OF THE COLOURS
MAY, HOWEVER, HAVE BEEN
ENHANCED AS THE RESULT
OF FADING OVER TIME.

FESTIVE APRON
Kaili City area, Qiandongnan Prefecture,
20th century

The base cloth of this rectangular front apron is
hand-woven cotton dyed dark indigo, on to which a
rectangular block of decoration has been sewn. This
consists of numerous strips of different-coloured
satins. Various coloured geometric motifs have been
stitched on to each strip with dark thread. Some
strips are edged with a folded, wafer-thin, malleable
'metal' strip, also attached by stitching.
44×47 cm ($17^{1}/_{4} \times 18^{1}/_{2}$ in)

THE OVERALL DESIGN IS BUILT UP FROM REPEATING STRIPS OF HIGHLY COLOURED MATERIAL, SUBTLY DECORATED. THIS INTRICACY CONTRASTS STRONGLY WITH THE BOLD,

ALMOST CRUDE, COLOURED 'SILK FELT' FRINGING AT THE BOTTOM OF THE APRON. TWO SINGLE ROWS OF METALLIC STRIPS BIND THE WARP THREADS.

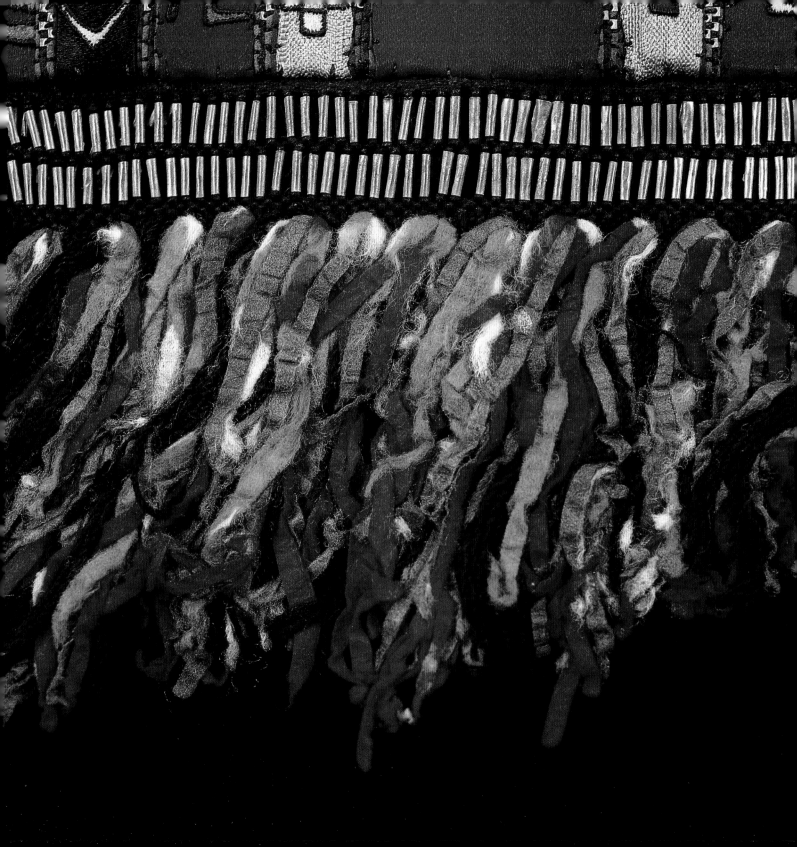

FEMALE FESTIVE JACKET (GEJIA GROUP)
Kaili City area, Qiandongnan Prefecture, 20th century

This slim-fitting long-sleeved jacket with stand-up collar and
front opening is made of cotton. It is decorated using the wax
resist technique and dyed in indigo.
82 × 136 cm (32 × 53¹⁄₂ in)

AN ELEGANT GARMENT
INCORPORATING TWO
CONTRASTING DESIGN
ELEMENTS: VERY BOLD
FOLIATE-PATTERNED
FRONT PANELS AND
SUBTLER GEOMETRICALLY
PATTERNED SLEEVE PANELS,
CLEVERLY INTERGATED
BY THE SIMPLEST USE OF
WHITE ON INDIGO.

FEMALE FESTIVE JACKET
Leishan and Taijiang County, Qiandongnan Prefecture,
20th century

The outer cloth of this sleeved, collared jacket is hand-woven
indigo-dyed cotton with an alternating float weave to give a
spiralling four-key design. The decoration,worked in satin
stitch, is applied to the sleeves, shoulders, collar and front
facings. The jacket has a front opening and side slits
94 × 124 cm (37 × 38³/₄ in)

A PERFECT EXAMPLE
OF FLAMBOYANT JACKET
DESIGN. THE CONCISE
TRADITIONAL COLLAR
DECORATION, CONSIST-
ING OF MANY LINES OF
FOLDED SILK TRIANGLES,
CONTRASTS WITH THE

EXUBERANT DESIGN ON
THE SLEEVES, DOMINATED
BY A BRIGHTLY COLOURED
DRAGON, WATER BUFFALO
AND BUTTERFLY INTER-
WOVEN WITH FLORAL
MOTIFS ON A DEEP BLUE
GROUND.

chapter 6

Textiles from Guatemala

Brocading detail from a young girl's *huipil*, made of cotton. The top third of the *huipil* is brocaded from selvedge to selvedge with small multicoloured diamonds, subdivided further into even smaller compartments, outlined in maroon and filled in using stranded cottons in a variety of soft colours. Nahualá. 60 x 57 cm (23$^1/_2$ x 22$^1/_2$ in).

HUIPIL
Quezaltenango

A woman's *huipil* made from three weft-faced panels sewn together.

Bands of *jaspe* patterns (dark blue and white) and supplementary weft
patterning (mauve and yellow) decorate the upper part of the garment.
The plain white portion underneath is tucked into the skirt.
106.5 × 120.5 cm (42 × 47 in)

THE DETAIL ILLUSTRATIONS SHOW A SPLENDID EMBROIDERED
RANDA THAT COVERS THE SEAM JOINING TWO OF THE PANELS,
DEPICTING LEAVES AND FLOWERS EITHER SIDE OF A TWISTING
STEM, AND A DELICATELY EMBROIDERED NECK OPENING THAT
INTRODUCES A CONTRASTING TOUCH OF NATURALISTIC COLOUR.

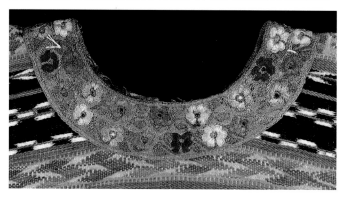

HAIR RIBBON
San Cristóbal Totonicapán

Long ribbons (*cintas*)
are wound into the hair in
many towns and villages.

These tapestry-woven
ribbons, in silk, cotton or
rayon, are finished with
pompoms connected by
wire-wrapped maguey
loops, ending in long
tassels. Laid out side
by side (right) are
different sections.
3.5 × 350 cm
(1³/₈ in × 11 ft 6 in)

THERE IS A STRUCTURE TO
THE ALL-OVER DESIGN OF
THE RIBBON THAT DERIVES
FROM THE FORMAL BANDS OF
COLOUR SEPARATING FIGUR-
ATIVE AND ABSTRACT FORMS.

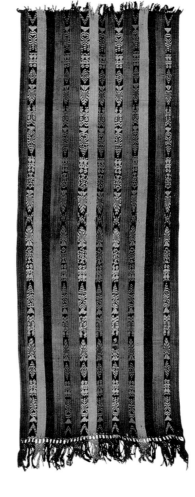

THE *JASPE* STRIPE (LEFT)
SHOWS TYPICAL PATTERNS
USED IN TIE-DYED WARPS –
FOR EXAMPLE, THE TWIN
FIGURES AND A PINE TREE.
THE BLURRED EDGES TO
THE DESIGNS ARE AN
INHERENT PART OF THE
IKAT PROCESS.

CEREMONIAL SHAWL (*PERRAJE*)
San Cristóbal Totonicapán

This shawl is worn either over
the shoulder or as a wrap.

Wide bands of muted coloured silk
alternate with bands of hand-spun cotton
jaspe thread. The knotted fringe shows
considerable signs of wear.
72 × 188 cm (28¹/₃ × 74 in)

HUIPIL
El Quiché, Chichicastenango

Huipil made up of three four-selvedge panels
of brown cotton, brocaded on the front, back and
shoulders, with a velvet trim neckline.

The wings and tail feathers of the double-headed
eagle on the central panel are represented by chevrons, a
feature repeated and exaggerated on the side panels.
70 × 81 cm (27¹/₂ × 32 in)

DETAIL OF THE CHEVRON AREA
OF THIS DESIGN SHOWS THAT
IT IS POSSIBLE EVEN WHEN
USING NUMEROUS VIBRANT
HUES TO ACHIEVE A HARMONY
BY CAREFULLY PLACING
EACH COLOUR BESIDE A
COMPLEMENTARY COLOUR.

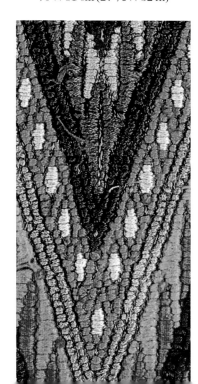

HUIPIL
El Quiché, Chichicastenango

Three-panel, four-selvedge, brown cotton
huipil brocaded in purple and pink silk floss, and
bright coloured stranded cottons.

The stylized eagle of the previous *huipil*
has given way to exuberant roses, converted from
printed cross stitch patterns to the typical raised
brocading technique of Chichicastenango.
66 × 100 cm (26 × 39¹/₃ in)

THE BOLD TWIST MOTIF
PROVIDES A FOCAL POINT ON
THE TWO SIDE PANELS. THIS,
TOGETHER WITH THE STRIPED
VERTICAL BARS OF THE *RANDAS*,
CONTRASTS THE ABSTRACT WITH
THE NATURALISTIC ELEMENTS OF
THE DESIGN.

TZUTE
El Quiché, Chichicastenango

Rectangular cloth used
as head-cloth, shawl, or cover

Originally woven in one long piece on the
back-strap loom, it was subsequently cut in half
and the pieces sewn together side by side, with
the fringes aligned at one end and the
raw edges hemmed at the other.
70 × 63.5 cm (27$^{1}/_{2}$ × 25 in)

THE WEAVER'S PERSONAL ADAPTATION OF THE POPULAR
DOLL FIGURE HAS BEEN TREATED IN A BOLD WAY.
YELLOW, ORANGE AND GREEN ACRYLICS HAVE BEEN
USED FOR THE DOUBLE-FACED BROCADING OVER THE
RED AND ORANGE STRIPED GROUND.

HERE THE IMAGERY IS DRAWN FROM A FOLK NARRATIVE. BECAUSE THE DESIGN IS WOVEN IN SINGLE-FACED BROCADING, WHERE NOTHING SHOWS ON THE REVERSE OF THE FABRIC, IT IS ALSO POSSIBLE TO ADMIRE THE CAREFUL ARRANGEMENT OF COLOURS IN THE STRIPED GROUND FABRIC.

FRINGED CLOTH (*TZUTE*)
El Quiché, Nebaj

Women wore this type of all-purpose cloth
folded on the head during *cofradía* ceremonies.

Made from a single striped panel, the *tzute*
is almost completely covered with rich brocading. The
ends are finished with decorative machine stitching
in white cotton, with the warp ends left as fringes.
75 cm (29 1/2 in) square, excluding fringes

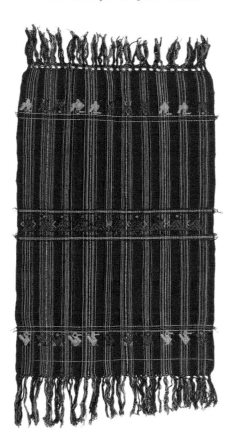

THE PROMINENT RED OF THE
WARP STRIPES CONTRASTS
BOLDLY WITH THE GREENS
OF THE BROCADING.

RED COTTON CLOTH
El Quiché, San Juan Cotzal

A shawl (*perraje*) or all-purpose cloth of red cotton striped
with many vibrant colours, with knotted fringes at each end.

Three bands of brocaded birds are contained within narrow
bands of supplementary weft, which extend in little tufts
similar to those on the Chajul sash.
77 × 52 cm (30¹/₄ × 20¹/₂ in) excluding fringe

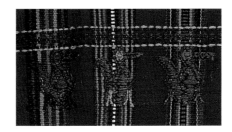

THIS WOVEN DESIGN SHOWS ALL THE SIGNS OF HAVING BEEN DESIGNED ON A MATRIX BUT IN FACT EXPLOITS THE 'STEP AND REPEAT' OF TWILL LINES. THIS, TOGETHER WITH THE FREQUENT CHANGES OF COLOUR, MAKES FOR A STRONG DESIGN.

FRINGED *TZUTE*
Sololá, Nahualá

Part of the men's costume, displaying zoomorphic motifs of exotic birds and animals within a frame of diamond frets.

Made from a single cotton panel of indigo-dyed ground with pairs of magenta warp-way stripes at intervals. The orange fringes have been knotted into the ends of the cloth.
75 × 61 cm (29$^1/_2$ × 24 in) excluding fringes.
Donated by Mrs Hazel Weymes

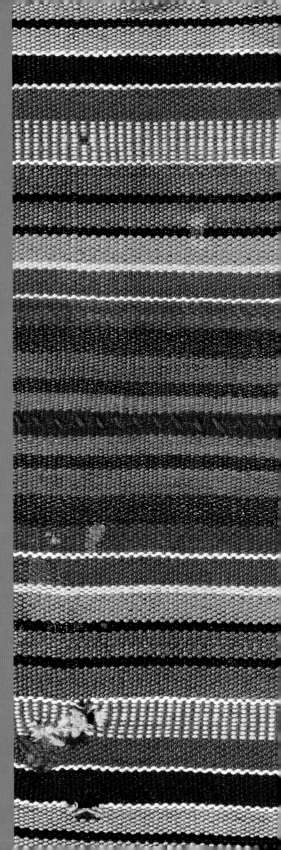

TZUTE
Sacatepéquez, San Antonio Aguas Calientes

Two-panel cloth worn folded on the
head or used as a utility cloth.

Weavers in this village are generally
acknowledged for their weaving expertise.
The motifs on the red ground between the striped
selvedges are worked in double-faced brocading,
a technique that resembles tapestry.
76 × 105 cm (30 × 41 in)

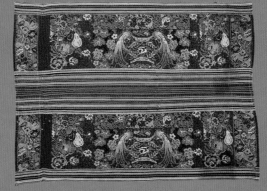

THE DESIGNS IN SAN ANTONIO CHANGED
IN THE 1960s WHEN WESTERN PATTERNS FOR
CROSS STITCH APPEARED. THE COMPLEXITY
OF THE SELVEDGES (STRIPES) CONTRASTS
STRIKINGLY WITH THE REALISM OF THE BIRDS,
FISHES AND FRUIT.

HUIPIL
Sacatepéquez, San Antonio Aguas Calientes

Beautifully woven two-panel, four-selvedge
huipil, displaying the many different designs in
the weaver's repertoire.

The figurative band is reserved for the part
that falls on to the shoulder. The non-figurative
bands, worked in a virtuoso display of different
techniques, use stranded brocading threads
in a large range of colours.
57×67 cm ($22^1/_2 \times 26^1/_3$ in)

THE USE OF A KALEIDOSCOPE OF COLOURS (EACH
REQUIRING A SEPARATE BROCADING THREAD), IS
PULLED TOGETHER VISUALLY BY THE MICROSCOPIC
APPEARANCE OF THE RED BINDING ENDS OF THE WARP
OVERLAYING THE BRIGHT COLOURS.

HUIPIL
San Raimundo Sacatepéquez

Two-panel *huipil* in distinctively coloured stripes of mauve, red, pale yellow and hand-spun natural brown cotton overlaid with exotic motifs.

Thick stranded threads are brocaded on a closed warp, giving two faces – positive on the front and negative on the back. There are similarities in colour and style with textiles from San Juan Sacatepéquez nearby. Both show fantastic creatures above, and below a motif variously called the 'feathered serpent' or 'rolling hills'.
66 × 109 cm (26 × 43 in)

THE STRENGTH OF THE
BROCADING COMBINES
TRIUMPHANTLY WITH THE
BOLD WARP STRIPES –
TO STUNNING EFFECT.

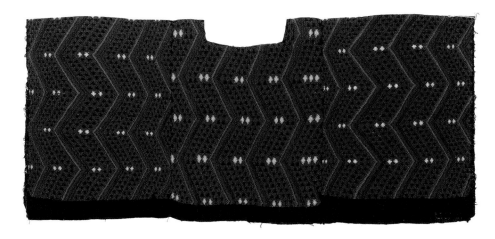

HUIPIL
Alta Verapaz, Tactic

The three panels of this everyday *huipil*
were woven separately, each with four selvedges.

The dark indigo ground, with its predominantly red
brocading, plays an important part in the decoration.
The dark triangles that follow the zigzag path
of the mauve and green lines (which at first glance
appear to be an addition) are actually the
ground weave, left unbrocaded.
43 × 101 cm (17 × 39¾ in)

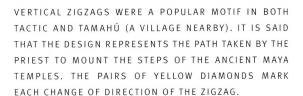

VERTICAL ZIGZAGS WERE A POPULAR MOTIF IN BOTH
TACTIC AND TAMAHÚ (A VILLAGE NEARBY). IT IS SAID
THAT THE DESIGN REPRESENTS THE PATH TAKEN BY THE
PRIEST TO MOUNT THE STEPS OF THE ANCIENT MAYA
TEMPLES. THE PAIRS OF YELLOW DIAMONDS MARK
EACH CHANGE OF DIRECTION OF THE ZIGZAG.

chapter 7

Textiles
from Mexico

Detail from an *ikat*-patterned silk rebozo woven on a backstrap loom and finished with braded warp-fringes. With Mexican *ikat*, only the warp is tie-dyed. Patterned before they are set up on the loom, warp threads are divided into sets. Each set is tightly bound and dyed separately to achieve the desired colour sequence. Indigo blue, pink, yellow and green are combined with the off-white of the undyed silk. Santa María del Rio, San Luis Potosí, 19th century. 235 x 72 cm (92^1/$_2$ x 28^1/$_2$ in). Donated by Lady Irene Logan.

THIS COMPLEX DESIGN INCORPORATES HORIZONTAL BANDS OF PICTORIAL MOTIFS WITHIN FORMAL BORDERS. THE SUBJECT MATTER IS REPEATED IN EVER-CHANGING COLOURS WITH SCANT REGARD FOR SCALE. DEER ARE THE SAME SIZE AS CHURCHES: HORSE RIDERS ARE HARDLY LARGER THAN ROSES. DESPITE THIS THE

BEDSPREAD HAS A STRONG VISUAL UNITY. THE WEAVING PROCESS, WHERE-BY THE WEFT INTERSECTS AT RIGHT ANGLES WITH THE WARP, DETERMINES THE ANGULAR APPEARANCE OF THESE BRO-CADED DESIGNS, ACHIEVED BY THE CAREFUL COUNTING OF THREADS. MOTIFS INTER-LOCK INGENIOUSLY ON A WHITE BACKGROUND.

BEDSPREAD
The Otomí, San Miguel Ameyalco, State of Mexico, 1977

Four-panel bedspread of white cotton brocaded with brightly coloured acrylic yarns.

Woven in four vertical panels on a backstrap loom by Ana Cecilia Cruz Alberto, this unusually large textile is weft-brocaded with a virtuoso display of birds, animals, flowers, churches and human figures. The exuberant design was inspired by the brocaded panels of cloth, termed *ayates*, that are worn by male dancers during local festivals.
The weaver works without a pattern.
282 × 265 cm (111 × 104¹/₂ in) excluding fringes

BLOUSE
The Otomí, San Pablito, Puebla, 1980s

Blouse of factory cotton cloth embroidered in pattern running
stitch with cotton thread.

In the Puebla highlands, blouses are unfitted. Fashioned from straight cloth panels, they
have square necklines and box-like sleeves. Each embroidered panel is worked separately.
When the blouse is assembled, the cloth below the yoke is gathered into tiny pleats. Cloth
joins are emphasized with decorative stitching. This fine example features geometric
designs and stylized plant motifs. This style of embroidery closely resembles brocading.
59 × 53 cm (23 × 21 in)

(OPPOSITE) EMBROIDERED SLEEVE PANELS DISPLAY THREE DIFFERENTLY
PATTERNED BANDS. A ZIGZAG LINE, INVERTED AT EACH APEX, SEPARATES THE
DESIGN UNITS. THESE ARE ALTERNATIVELY REVERSED AS THEY TRAVEL ALONG
EACH BAND. THE SYMMETRY IS ENHANCED BY THE USE OF A SINGLE COLOUR
THAT STANDS OUT AGAINST THE WHITE BASE CLOTH.

EMBROIDERED CLOTH
The Otomí, Tenango de Doria, Hidalgo, *c.* 1977

Factory cloth embroidered in satin stitch
with mercerized cotton thread.

For several decades, Otomí women in Tenango de Doria
and San Pablito have earned much-needed revenue by
embroidering imaginative and often fantastical landscapes.
This example displays a wealth of plant
designs and hybrid creatures.
152 × 107 cm (60 × 42 in)

THE APPARENT SIMPLICITY AND 'NAIVE' CHARM OF THIS WORK ARE
DECEPTIVE. IT TAKES ENORMOUS SKILL TO POSITION RANDOM
FIGURES IN SPACE, YET ACHIEVE AN OVERALL SENSE OF BALANCE
AND HARMONY.

EMBROIDERED CLOTH
The Otomí, Tenango de Doria, Hidalgo, *c.* 1977

Factory cloth embroidered with a vibrant and highly decorative landscape in satin stich, with mercerized cotton thread.

Before starting work, most women draw the outline of their designs freehand on to the cloth with a ballpoint pen. Although some stitches are very long, this is an economical form of satin stich because threads travel back across the surface – not the underside – of the cloth.
180 × 72$\frac{1}{2}$ cm (71 × 28$\frac{1}{2}$ in)

BOLDLY EXECUTED RED AND BLACK MOTIFS ARE ASYMMETRICALLY POSITIONED TO FORM A HUMOROUS YET HARMONIOUS COMPOSITION. THIS DESIGN IS A UNIQUE CREATION ALTHOUGH THE TYPES OF ELEMENTS USED HERE ARE FOUND ON MANY SUCH CLOTHS.

BLOUSE
The Nahua, Naupan, 1980s

Blouse of factory cotton cloth embroidered with blue
artifical silk yarn and red cotton thread.

Fashioned from straight cloth panels, this blouse
combines two distinct styles of decoration. Blue areas
have been hand-embroidered in pattern running stitch
to show birds, animals and flowers. Red areas have
been patterned on a sewing machine to display
spirals, leaves and other organic forms. A
frill has been added below the yoke.
70 × 68 cm (27^{1}/$_{2}$ × 27 in)

THE EMBROIDERY IS SO DENSE THAT THE FEW
WHITE AREAS THAT REMAIN CREATE THE DESIGN.

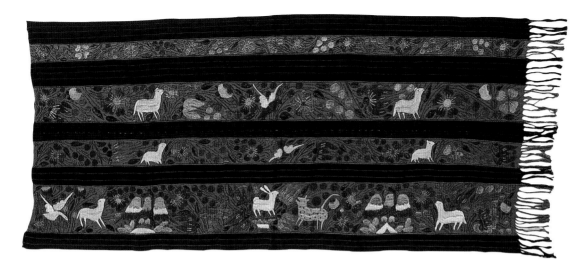

THIS SKIRT ABOUNDS WITH CHARMING ANIMALS, BIRDS AND FLOWERS. IT ALSO INCLUDES MEXICO'S
NATIONAL EMBLEM, SHOWN TWICE ALONG THE LOWER BAND, IN THE FORM OF AN EAGLE, PERCHED ON A
PRICKLY PEAR, WITH A SERPENT IN ITS BEAK.

WRAP-AROUND SKIRT
The Nahua, Acatlán, Guerrero, 1970s

Embroidered wrap-around skirt, woven in two panels on a backstrap loom with indigo-dyed cotton.

The skirt has pale blue and dark blue warp bands. Pale blue bands carry a wealth of designs
bordered by the dark blue bands. The embroiderer has used synthetic silk thread and a combination of
satin and couching techniques. For extra show, women sometimes add sequins, which glint in the sunshine.
On weekdays, many women protect this delicate embroidery by wearing their skirts wrong-side out.
218 × 99 cm (86 × 39 in)

SARAPE
Possibly from Saltillo, Coahuila, 19th century

Saltillo-style *sarape*, woven in two panels on
a treadle loom with a wool weft.

.

Tapestry weaving gives this *sarape* its distinctive
patterning. During the colonial period, Saltillo
became the most famous production centre.
Later the term 'Saltillo' was applied to similarly
patterned *sarapes* from other towns. This fine
example displays small lozenges and
other interlocking geometric elements grouped
round a diamond centre. When the *sarape* is
worn, the patterning is vertical.
224 × 116 cm (88 × 45$^{1}/_2$ in)

BY MANIPULATING RICHLY COLOURED THREADS,
TAPESTRY-WEAVERS ACHIEVED DAZZLING MOSAIC
EFFECTS DESCRIBED BY NÁHUATL-SPEAKERS AS
ACOCEMALOTIC-TILMATLI (RAINBOW-MANTLES).

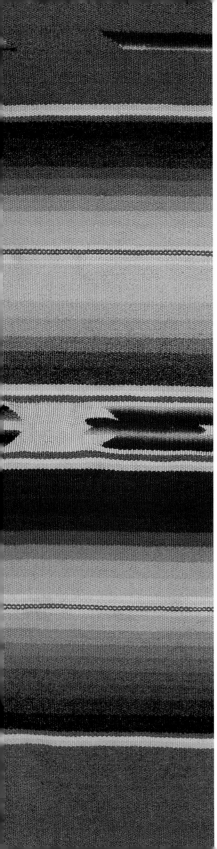
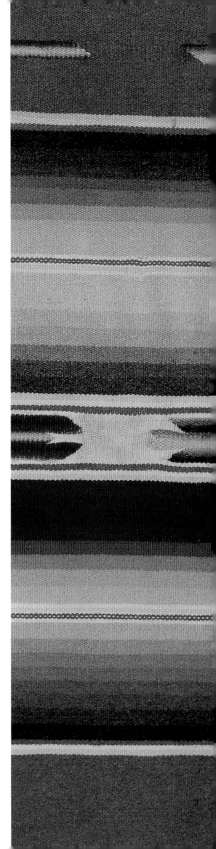

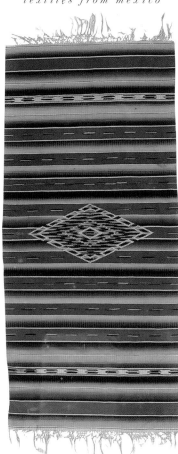

SARAPE
Aguascalientes-style, tapestry-patterned *sarape*,
probably late 19th century

Woven as a single panel on a treadle loom with shaded
wool, the *sarape* has a short finger-knotted warp fringe.

Yarn was delicately shaded for the weft stripes by
a process known as *ombré* dyeing. Each skein
was dipped in a colour, dried off, then partially
re-dipped in a stronger solution. Successive
dippings produced the desired shading.
196 × 91 cm (77 × 36 in) excluding fringes

IN THIS EXAMPLE THE LOZENGE PLAYS A LESS
IMPORTANT ROLE IN THE OVERALL DESIGN, ALLOWING
THE BACKGROUND TO HAVE A POWERFUL IMPACT.

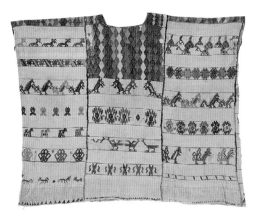

HUIPIL (FRONT AND BACK)
The Mixtec, San Miguel Metlatonoc, Guerrero, 1970s

Three-panel gala *huipil,* woven on a backstrap loom from
hand-spun cotton. Designs are brocaded with commercial cotton thread.

Brightly coloured brocaded motifs include geometric elements, birds
with outstretched wings, double-headed eagles, and rearing horses with
plumed tails (see detail below). Interlocking diamond motifs pattern the
shoulder line and part of the central panel. Much-worn, this *huipil* has
been reinforced at the neck with a narrow section of embroidered cloth.
Panels are joined with decorative insertion stitching.
79 × 98 cm (31 × 38¹/₂ in)

THIS SPLENDID AND HIGHLY DECORATED GARMENT IS UNUSUAL IN THAT IT HAS BEEN WOVEN WITH
ALMOST NO REGARD FOR SYMMETRY. EACH PANEL HAS BEEN CONCEIVED INDIVIDUALLY.

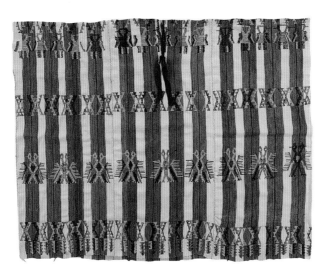

HUIPIL
The Mixtec, San Pedro Jicayàn, Oaxaca, early 1970s

Three-panel *huipil* with brocaded motifs, woven on a backstrap loom.

The weaver has used hand-spun white cotton, lilac cotton dyed with the secretion of shellfish, and *hiladillo* (cochineal-dyed silk). The neck opening is edged in satin ribbon. Such garments are worn for the marriage ceremony or by the wives of dignitaries.
104 × 133 cm (41 × 52¹/₂ in)

THE STRENGTH OF THIS DESIGN LIES IN ITS USE OF SYMMETRY
WITH STYLIZED BROCADED MOTIFS RUNNING HORIZONTALLY
ACROSS THE WARP BANDS. MOTIFS INCLUDE TWO VERSIONS
OF DOUBLE-HEADED BIRDS (BELOW AND RIGHT)

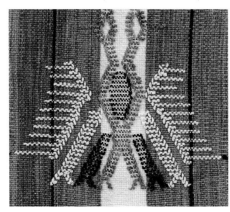

HUIPIL
The Mazatec, San Bartolomé Ayautla,
Oaxaca, before 1913

This richly embroidered cotton *huipil*
has a square-cut opening for the head.

In recent decades, the *huipiles* of the Mazatec have
increasingly been made from factory cloth. This magnificent
old-style *huipil*, however, is plain- and gauze-woven on a
backstrap loom in two panels. It features a wide band of
brocading along the bottom.
84 × 92 cm (33 × 36 in)

CURVILINEAR BIRDS, RABBITS AND LUSH PLANT DESIGNS HAVE BEEN EMBROIDERED WITH PATTERN DARNING STITCH AND OUTLINE STITCH, CREATING TWO DIFFERENT EFFECTS. THE UPPER USES THE WHITE BASE CLOTH TO DRAW THE OUTLINE OF THE PLANT AND BIRDS, WHEREAS THE LOWER ROW OF BIRDS USES A SIMPLE SILHOUETTE TECHNIQUE. THE BROCADED BORDER, WORKED IN A DIFFERENT STYLE, IS MADE UP OF STYLIZED PLANTS AND GEOMETRIC REPEAT PATTERNING.

HUIPIL
The Chinantec, San Felipe Usila, Oaxaca

Child's knee-length *huipil* of cotton and artificial silk,
woven in three panels on a backstrap loom, and partially overpainted.

In traditional communities, children's clothing is similar to that worn by adults.
Vivid clusters of weft stripes alternate with rows of raised geometric motifs brocaded
on to a white ground of plain and gauze weave. The round neckline is reinforced with
decorative stitching. *Appliquéd* ribbon and braid are used to conceal the panel joins.
87×65 cm ($34^{1}/_{2} \times 25^{1}/_{2}$ in)

WOMEN IN SAN FELIPE USILA
LIKE TO PAINT OVER SELECTED
AREAS OF THEIR ORNATE
HUIPILES WITH AN ANILINE
DYE CALLED *FUCHINA*.

INTRICATELY WOVEN DESIGNS
ARE GIVEN A COAT OF MUTED
PURPLE TO STOP THE SUN
FROM 'EATING THE COLOUR OF
THE THREADS'.

HUIPIL
The Chinantec, San Lucas Ojitlán, Oaxaca, 1970s

Embroidered cotton *huipil*,
woven in three panels on a backstrap loom.

Bold designs, embroidered in pattern running stitch, dominate areas
of white gauze-woven ground bordered by colourful weft stripes. Cloth panels
are joined with vertical bands of decorative stitching; arm openings are trimmed
to resemble sleeves with crocheted lace and ribbon. Before the Conquest, Mexican
huipiles often displayed a small rectangle in the centre of the chest. Here, a tiny
section of *appliquéd* ribbon perpetuates this ancient custom.
90 × 92 cm (35^1/$_2$ × 36 in)

DESIGNS ARE ORGANIZED WITH NEAR PERFECT SYMMETRY – ONLY THE COLOUR OF THE CENTRAL STRIPES BREAKS THE SYMMETRY. THE STYLIZED DOUBLE-HEADED BIRDS,

WIDELY THOUGHT TO BE A PRE-CONQUEST SURVIVAL, HAVE THE APPEARANCE OF BROCADED MOTIFS. AS WITH MANY MEXICAN TEXTILES, RED IS THE DOMINANT COLOUR.

chapter 8

Textiles from the Andes

Detail from a loincloth. The plain-weave double cloth has a main design of
repeated felines. Bands of complementary-weft weave in red and yellow
camelid fibre yarns stand out against the plain cloth and blue patterns. The
cotton yarns in natural white and dyed blue are matt in comparison with the
glossy camelid fibre pile on p. 289. AD 1000–1476. 102.5 x 26.5 cm
(40 ^{1}/$_3$ x 10^1/$_2$ in). Given by Sir Patrick Manson.

BORDER FROM AN EMBROIDERED MANTLE
Paracas, 200 BC–AD 600

Birds, with outstretched wings and hexagonal eyes, are embroidered in
stem stitch against a solid red ground on a yellow plain-weave fabric.
Inside the border is a row of birds with large, heart-shaped heads. In this
block colour style, the embroiderer first outlined the motif and then filled
in the background with diagonally oriented lines of stitches.
24.5 × 103 cm (9²/₃ × 40¹/₂ in)
Given by Henry van den Burgh through The Art Fund

THE PROMINENT EYES AND THE HEART-SHAPED FACES ARE REMINISCENT OF
BARN OWLS. THESE BIRDS SEEM TO HAVE A MYTHICAL STATUS; THEY SHARE
THE WHISKERS ALSO SPORTED BY FELINES WITH SIMILAR CONCENTRIC EYES
ON OTHER ANDEAN TEXTILES.

TASSEL
Nasca, 200 BC–AD 600

Different techniques in this tassel create a diamond pattern in oblique interlacing and staggered horizontal bands of plain weave, with motifs executed in complementary-warp weave in which the unused colours float between the layers.

35 × 22 cm (13 3/4 × 8 2/3 in)

THE TASSEL'S HEAD IS WOVEN IN COMPLEMENTARY-WARP WEAVE ORIENTED AT NINETY DEGREES TO THE MAIN PART.

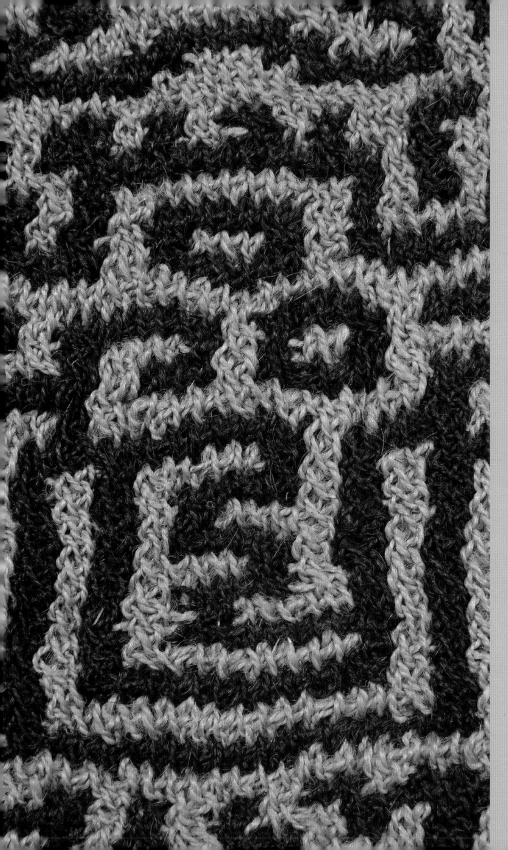

TASSEL

Nasca, 200 BC–AD 600

This tassel was worked in oblique intertwining (sprang), in which the interchanging of yarns in two colours at one end of the fabric produced a design in mirror-image at the other end.

32 × 23 cm (12$\frac{1}{2}$ × 9 in)

THE FABRIC WAS THEN FOLDED WHERE THE TWO ENDS OF THE DESIGN MEET AND A TASSEL HEAD, STITCHED IN CROSS-KNIT LOOPING, COVERS THIS FOLD.

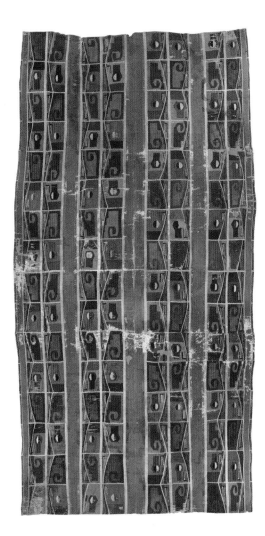

TAPESTRY TUNIC
Wari, 600–1000

This tunic was woven on a wide loom; the complete illustration shows it with the side
seams unstitched. The warp is undyed cotton and the weft is both undyed and dyed
camelid fibre. Two design units alternate. White dividing lines separate a stylized feline
head, with crossed fangs and a two-colour split eye, from a stepped and coiled tail motif.
207 × 107 cm (81^1/$_2$ × 42^1/$_4$ in)

A CURIOUS CHARACTERISTIC OF WARI TAPESTRIES IS THE ALTERNATING
EXPANSION AND CONTRACTION OF THE DESIGN UNITS, AS SEEN ON THE LEFT.

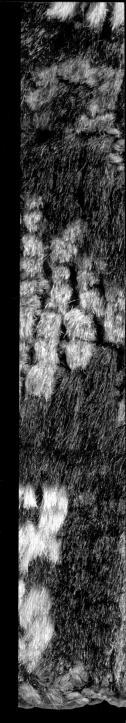

FOUR-CORNERED HAT
Wari, 600–1000

This hat is constructed from a continuous yarn in compactly
worked larkshead knots into which coloured threads were inserted
to form a pile. Geometric designs with little squares containing a
dot in the middle are characteristic of such hats.
11 × 12 cm (4¹/3 × 4³/4 in)

THE LUXURIANT CUT PILE IN RICH DYED AND UNDYED
NATURAL COLOURS DEMONSTRATES THE GLOSSINESS OF
CAMELID FIBRE.

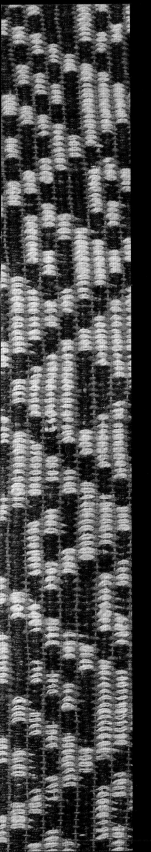

THE PATTERN MOTIFS OF THIS ALL-COTTON TEXTILE WERE FORMED
FROM HORIZONTALLY ALIGNED 3-SPAN FLOATS IN A WEAVE DERIVED
FROM 2/1 TWILL.

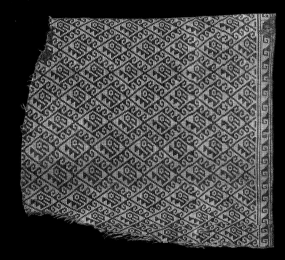

TEXTILE FRAGMENT
Chancay, 1000–1476

The natural brown warp and weft are finer than the white and
blue warps, which dominate the surface of the textile in a handsome
design based on a bird and wave motif.
65.5 × 81.5 cm (25³/₄ × 32¹/₄ in)

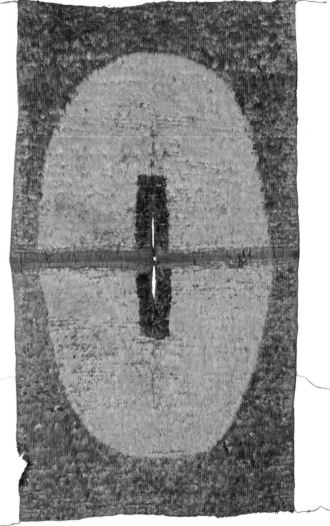

THE FEATHERS POSSIBLY COME FROM BLUE-AND-
YELLOW MACAWS, IN WHICH CASE THEY WOULD
HAVE BEEN OBTAINED FROM AMAZONIA.

TUNIC
Pre-Hispanic, period and culture unknown

A tunic woven from cotton in plain weave
has rows of feathers sewn to it.
141 × 80 cm (55$^1/_2$ × 31$^1/_2$ in)
Given by John Goble

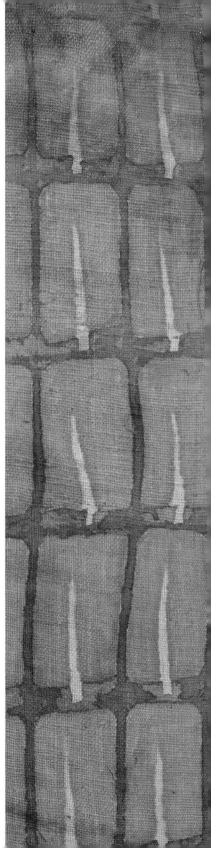

THE TUNIC IS SHOWN OPENED OUT. WHEN WORN,
THE CIRCLES WOULD HAVE BEEN ON ONE SIDE (FOR
EXAMPLE, THE FRONT) AND THE FEATHERS ON THE
OTHER SIDE (THE BACK).

TUNIC
1000–1476

An all-cotton plain weave tunic was painted on
one side with a design of circles and dots, with
a running scroll design at the bottom (see p. 291).
The other side was painted with rows of
feathers (see p. 292).
111 × 67 cm (43³/₄ × 26¹/₂ in)

SLING
Pre-Hispanic, period and culture unknown

The sling has a ribbed cradle, with a central slit. The cradle's borders
have decorative stitching in alternating blocks of colour.
181.5 × 5.2 cm (71$\frac{1}{2}$ × 2$\frac{1}{4}$ in). Given by John Goble

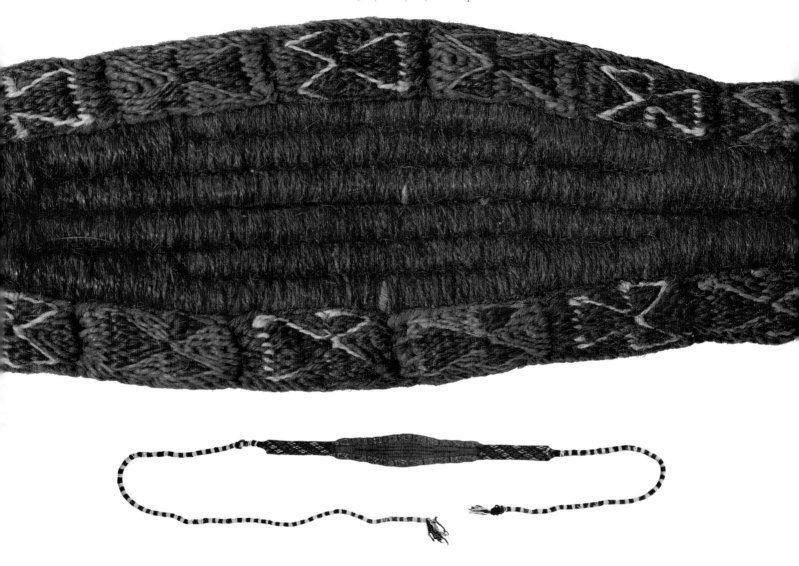

THE PLAITED SECTIONS EACH SIDE OF THE CRADLE END IN
CORDS, WHICH ARE WRAPPED IN BLACK AND WHITE YARNS.

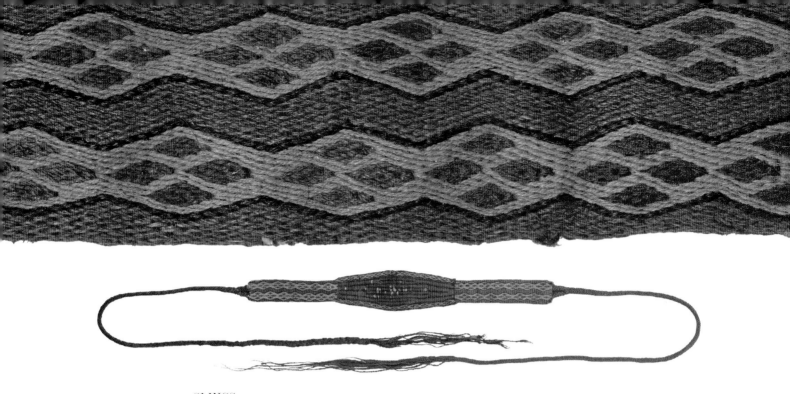

SLINGS
Pre-Hispanic, period and culture unknown

These slings are ceremonial examples of a tool used in everyday life –
in herding and to scare birds away from seed crops – and in warfare to
pound an enemy into defeat. Above: 308 × 8 cm (121¼ × 3¼ in);
below: 174 × 2.5 cm (68½ × 1 in). Given by John Goble

THE DETAIL ABOVE SHOWS THE PLAITING AT THE
END OF THE CRADLE. THE DETAIL BELOW
FOCUSES ON THE WEFT-WRAPPED CRADLE.

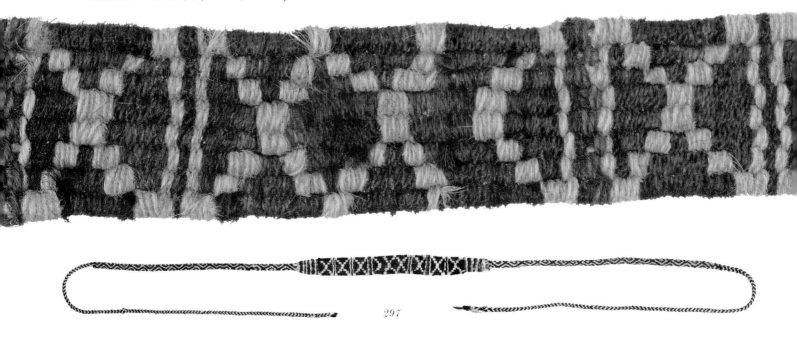

LOOM LENGTH
AD 1000–1476

The figure of a standing personage is executed in double weave, which means
that it appears in blue on a tan ground on the reverse. In the plain weave area
with the horizontal lines, the weaver used alternating blue and tan wefts to
correspond with the colour of the warp.

44.5 × 21.5 cm ($17^{1}/_{2}$ × $8^{1}/_{2}$ in)

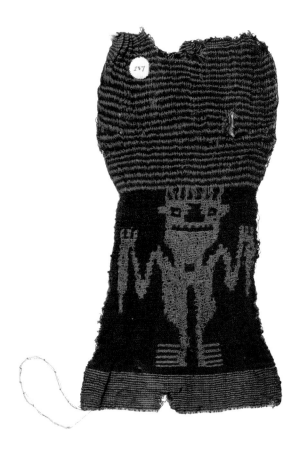

THIS TEXTILE IS CHARACTERISTIC OF ANDEAN
WEAVING BECAUSE IT HAS FOUR SELVEDGES: TWO
SIDE SELVEDGES FORMED BY THE TURNS OF THE
WEFT AND TWO END SELVEDGES FORMED BY THE
TURNS OF THE WARP.

FRAGMENT OF MANTLE OR DRESS
Chuquibamba, 1476–1534

This fragment was woven in tapestry in which the weft yarns interlock where
one colour yarn meets another. The boxes contain a pattern woven from
complementary weft weave with the unused colours floating on the back of
the fabric, creating a textile with right and wrong faces.
48.5 × 57.5 cm (19 1/4 × 22 3/4 in)
Given by the Wellcome Historical
Medical Museum

THE FIGURED AND TABBED BOXES IN THE DESIGN ARE
REPEATED IN A DIAGONAL COLOUR ARRANGEMENT.

HEAD COVERING
Chancay, 1000 – 1476

This gauze weave textile has a mesh of open squares which
were embroidered to produce the design. The warp, weft and
embroidery threads are of fine, tightly spun cotton, but the mouth
and eyes of the felines were embroidered using a heavier thread.
The finished piece was tie-dyed.
89 × 92 cm (35 × 36$^{1}/_{4}$ in)

THIS TEXTILE PROBABLY COVERED THE HEAD OF A MUMMY BUNDLE IN
A TOMB ON THE CENTRAL COAST OF PERU.

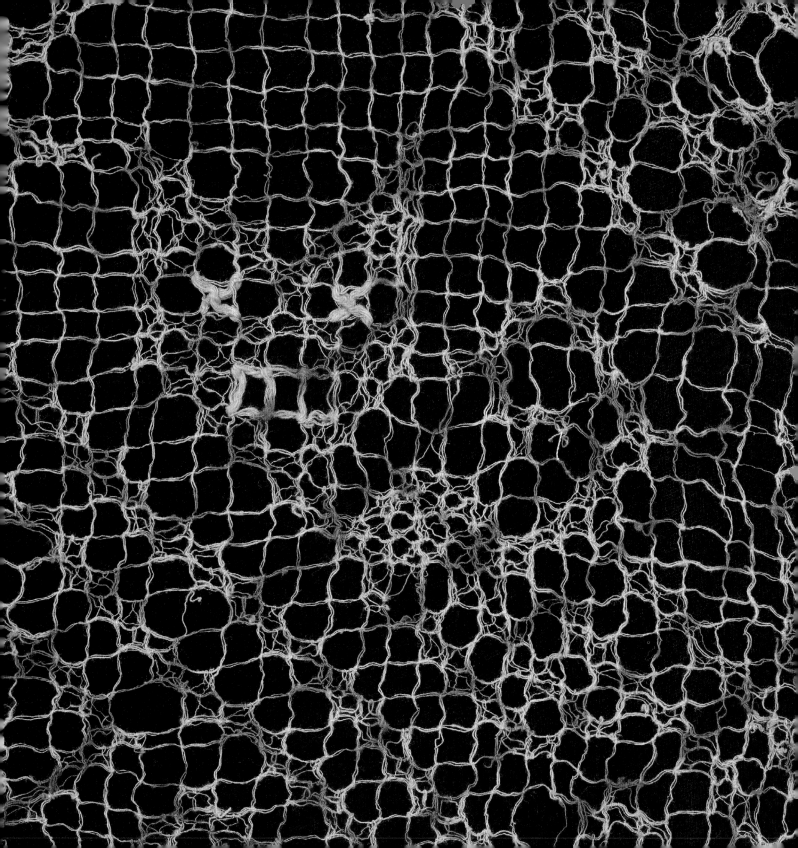

SHAWL
16th–19th century

This tapestry-woven shawl has interlocked wefts where one colour meets
another, a structure with a long tradition in the Andes (see pp. 287 and 300).
Motifs introduced into the Andes from Europe and the Far East are
worked into the broad tapestry bands.
98 × 130 cm (38 2/3 × 51 1/4 in).
Given by Miss Emily A. E. Shirreff

NARROW BANDS OF COMPLEMENTARY-WEFT WEAVE CREATE DESIGNS OF LITTLE BLOCKS AND
ZIGZAGS. THE BLOCKS BELOW INCORPORATE INKA MOTIFS.

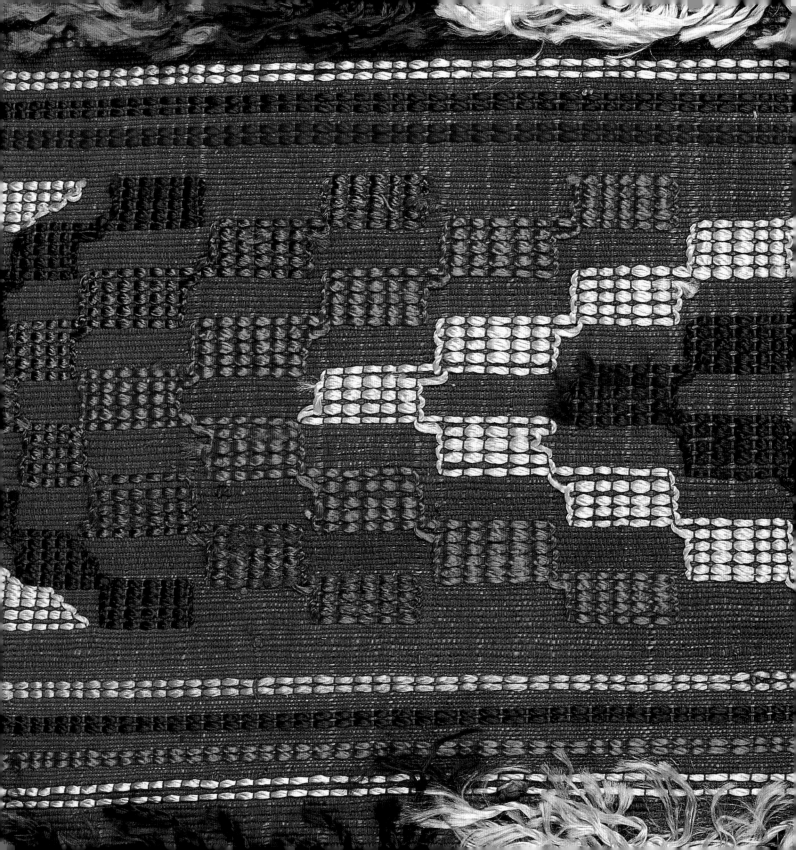

chapter 9

Silk in Africa

Detail from a ceremonial cloth (*itagbe*) made by the Yoruba people. Women
produce these ceremonial cloths which are worn by chiefs of the Ogboni
society. The cotton base is decorated with silk. The bold, tactile design uses
vibrant colours. It is organized into tufted sections (*shaki*) separated by
stepped geometric outer panels. The tufts have protective qualities.
Ijebu-ode, Nigeria. 151 x 42 cm (59^1/$_2$ x 16^1/$_2$ in).

CEREMONIAL DRESS
(ASHERIN NABIYAD)
Siwa Oasis, Egypt, late 20th century

The white dress is traditionally reserved
for use by the bride on the third day of the
wedding celebrations.

This dress is made of rayon, but formerly
such garments would have been made of white silk.
Women sew amulets onto the dress to protect the bride
from malevolent forces. Here we see shiny mother-of-
pearl buttons, known locally as the 'eye of the sun'. The
cowrie shells ensure the bride's fertility.
122 × 184 cm / 48 × 72 ins

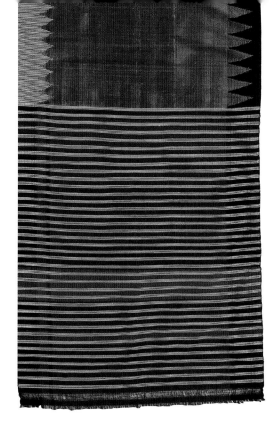

WOMAN'S MODESTY GARMENT
Egypt, late 20th century

Women wrap this cloth around the head and body
while outside the home.

This tapestry-woven rayon wrap developed from the silk and cotton garments
once woven by men for sale to women of the Bahariya Oasis. Such cloths are now
produced by women using treadle looms. The shimmering cloth conceals the
identity of the woman, but artful draping may reveal the body form.
424 × 77 cm (67 × 30¼ in)

THE COMBINATION OF OPPOSING COLOURED THREADS —
BLUE-GREEN AND MAGENTA — ENHANCES THE SURFACE
SHIMMER EFFECT.

WOMAN'S SHAWL
(*TANSHIFA*)
Algiers, Algeria, 19th century

Reserved for use by wealthy women at home.

This shawl is exquisitely worked,
predominantly in violet silk thread, on fine cotton.
The principal foliage motifs, worked in Algerian star stitch,
are derived from Italian Renaissance forms. Horizontal bands of
fine needlework in gold-coloured silk thread separate the
bolder elements of decoration.
286 × 40 cm (112$^1/_2$ × 15$^3/_4$ in)
Donated by Mrs Eustace Smith

THE BOLD, VIOLET PATTERNS ARE
BEAUTIFULLY BALANCED BY TINY, DELICATE
FLORAL MOTIFS SCATTERED THROUGHOUT.

CEREMONIAL BELT
Fès, Morocco

Such belts were used by women on ceremonial occasions.
They were worn folded in half and wrapped several times around the *qaftan*.

Woven on a draw loom, complex patterns were produced using supplementary
heddles. The two sections below show the wide variety of colour and design
combinations made possible through using this technique. This is a versatile belt
and can be folded to display different patterns for different occasions.
231 × 17 cm (91 × 6³/₄ in).

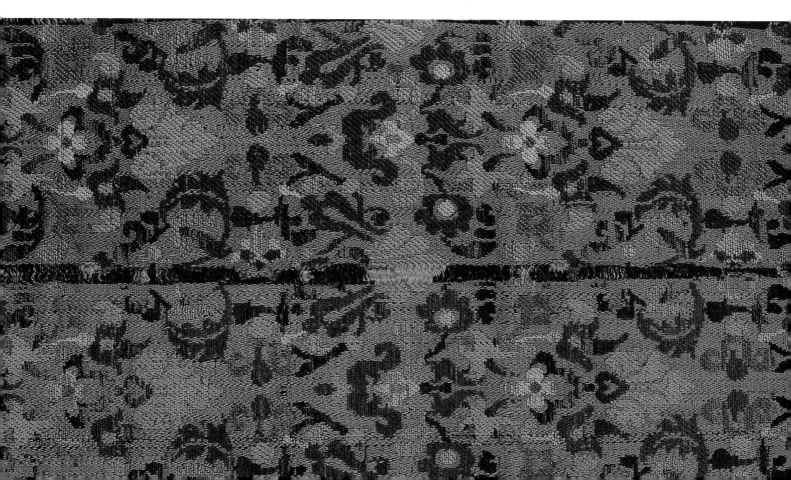

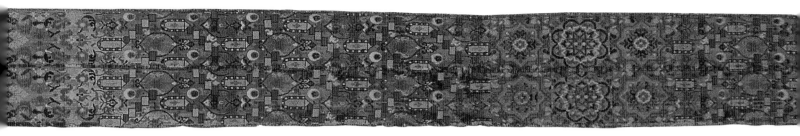

THE GEOMETRIC HERALDIC MOTIFS OF HISPANIC-MORESQUE INSPIRATION
CONTRACT WITH THE MORE FLUID, FLORAL MOTIFS INSPIRED BY LATER
EUROPEAN AND TURKISH DESIGNS. THE USE OF THE SAME COLOUR PALETTE
THROUGHOUT UNITES ALL THE DISPARATE ELEMENTS. THE BASE CLOTH
CHANGES FROM BLUE TO GREEN AT THE CENTRE TO PRODUCE TOTALLY
DIFFERENT EFFECTS WITHIN THE SAME BELT.

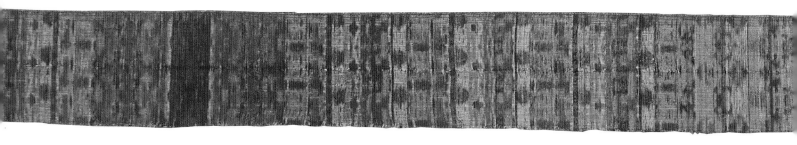

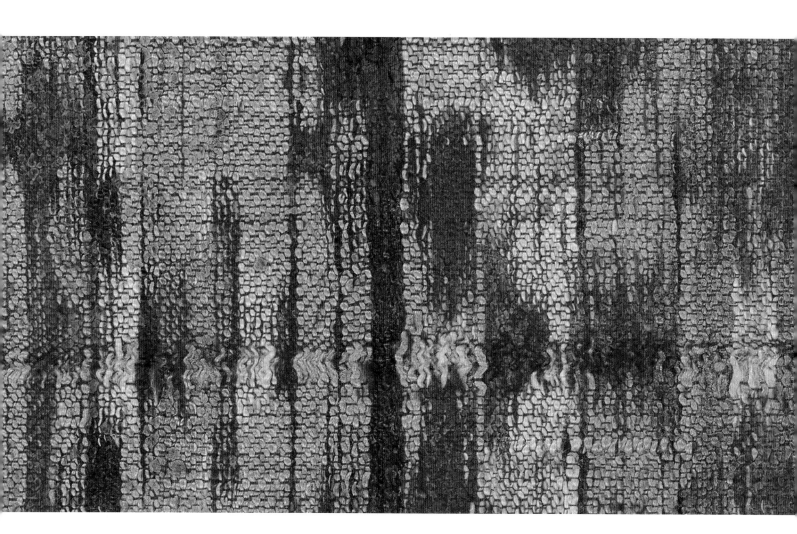

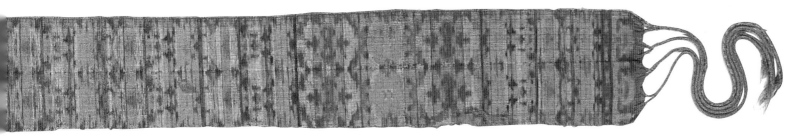

THE FORMAL DESIGNS ON THE FRONT OF THIS BELT
PRODUCE A STUNNING ABSTRACT PATTERN ON THE REVERSE.
THE *IKAT* WEAVE IS VISUALLY STRIKING.

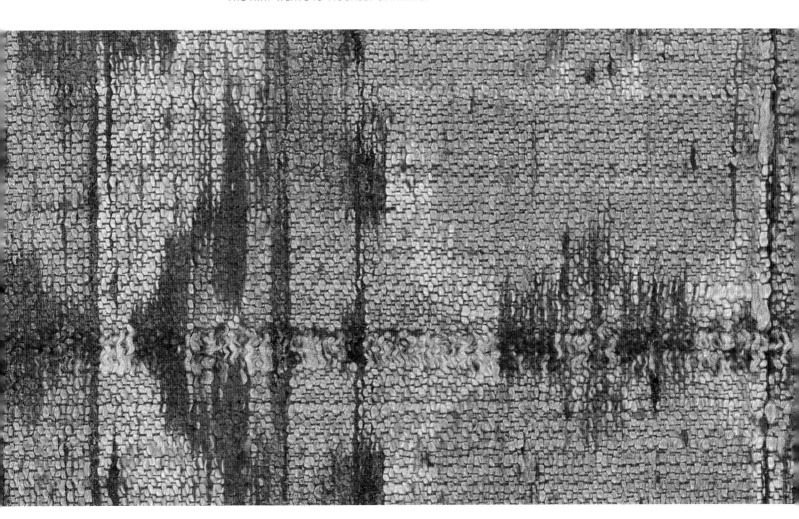

WOMAN'S VEIL (*RIDA'*)
Tunisia, 19th century

Head-veils were worn by elite women in 19th-century
Tunisia when outside the home.

Supplementary heddles are used to produce the complex patterns,
which include the 'eight-pointed star' – one of the most common motifs used
by Muslims in North Africa. Hand motifs (*khamsa*) of various forms also
feature regularly, as well as stylized carnations, derived from
Turkey, and cypress trees inspired by the Levant.
278 × 55 cm (109$^{1}/_{2}$ × 21$^{1}/_{2}$ in). Donated by Mrs Eustace Smith

THIS FORMAL DESIGN IS ACHIEVED USING THREE
STYLES OF STRIPES, WHERE THE MOST COMPLEX
BECOMES THE DOMINANT FEATURE.

ON A LAVISH BACKGROUND OF DAZZLING TURQUOISE SILK, THIS WAISTCOAT IS DECORATED WITH MOTIFS OF FISH, FLOWERS, STARS, CRESCENTS AND BIRDS THOUGHT TO ENSURE FERTILITY AND TO BRING GOOD LUCK.

THE BACK AND FRONT ARE EQUALLY FLAMBOYANT: 'WINGED' SHOULDERS OF TURKISH INSPIRATION GIVE THE WAISTCOAT ADDED SHAPE; GLITTERING SEQUINS AND INTRICATE GOLD EMBROIDERY ADD RICHNESS.

WOMAN'S WAISTCOAT (*FARMLA*)
Raf-raf, Tunisia, 20th century

Such waistcoats are often worn at marriages and other special occasions.

This waistcoat would have been embroidered by the bride or the female members of her family. It has a deeply scooped neckline, designed to reveal the richly decorated panel of the tunic or blouse worn underneath. The designs are worked in coiled gold and coloured metal thread and sequins. Tiny coral beads are sewn to the front of the waistcoat; in the Mediterranean coral is associated with fertility. 40 × 45 cm (15³/₄ × 17³/₄ in). Purchased with assistance from British Petroleum.

THE STRIKING GRAPHIC
FIGURES REPRESENT KING
BAKAFFA'S BODY ON A
FUNERAL BIER, FLANKED BY
ANGELS WITH STYLIZED
WINGS (LEFT). THE DOMINANT
RED AND ORANGE COLOURING
HAS BEEN ENLIVENED BY
THE INTRODUCTION OF BLUE
AND GREEN LINES.

HANGING SCREEN
Ethiopia, mid-18th century

This textile was once part of a triptych, designed to separate
the inner sanctum from the main body of a church.

This is the largest tablet-woven textile in the
world and is woven entirely of imported Chinese silk on a
tablet-weaving loom. The design probably represents
a funerary procession with figures arranged in descending
hierarchy: at the top is the body of King Bakaffa, followed by
his wife Queen Mentuab, his son Iyasu, and then clerics,
governors and soldiers.
306 × 63 cm (20^1/$_2$ × 24^3/$_4$ in).

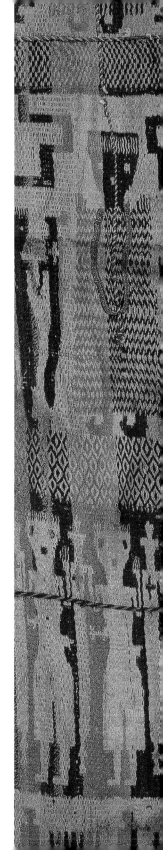

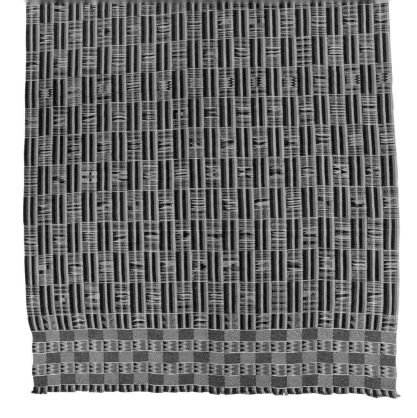

SILK AND COTTON WRAP
Ghana, 20th century

Worn by men, draped around the body and over the left shoulder and arm.

This cloth made by the Asante people is composed of twenty-four narrow strips woven by men using a double-heddle loom. The strips are sewn together to produce a magnificent overall effect. Bold warp stripes in yellow, green, red and blue combine with weft-float pattens.
306 × 183 cm (104 1/2 × 72 in)
Donated by Charles A. Beving

A VARIETY OF WEFT-FLOAT DESIGNS ALTERNATE WITH THE SIMPLE WARP STRIPES TO CREATE A REGULARLY SPACED AND BALANCED COMPOSITION.

THE BLUE IN THE MAIN DESIGN IS HIDDEN IN THE BORDER, WITH ITS DISTINCTIVE BUT COMPARITIVELY SIMPLE ALTERNATING PATTERN.

THIS IS AN INTENSELY PATTERNED, DYNAMIC TEXTILE WHICH JUXTAPOSES COLOUR AND DESIGN.

THE NON-ALIGNMENT OF THE PATTERN ELEMENTS ADDS TO THE SENSE OF MOTION AND VIBRANCY.

COTTON AND SILK CLOTH
Ewe people, Ghana, 19th century

The warp stripes of this cloth alternate with
weft-faced blocks in machine-spun cotton, embellished with
supplementary weft floats in silk. There are seven different patterns
of warp stripes as well as numerous weft-faced designs. It uses ready-
dyed machine-spun cotton, which provides a wider range of colours
than cotton that has been locally spun and dyed.
278 × 189 cm (109$^{1}/_{2}$ × 74$^{1}/_{2}$ in)
Donated by Charles A. Beving

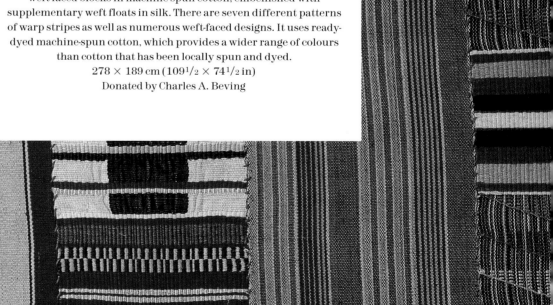

MAN'S ROBE
Probably Hausa or Nupe people, northern Nigeria

This prestigious robe would have been worn on special occasions.

It is woven in narrow strips using white and indigo-dyed cotton
to produce a distinctive pattern known as the 'guineafowl' design. It is
embroidered using imported silk thread. The right-hand side of the front of
this robe is dominated by an expanded form of the 'eight-knives' pattern.
Its intricate embroidery extends almost to the hem of the garment.
148 × 260 cm (58$^1/_4$ × 102$^1/_2$ in)
Donated by Charles A. Beving

THE 'TRIPLE BARB' (*GABIYA*)
PATTERN IS CHARACTERISTIC
OF NUPE EMBROIDERY AND
IS PARTICULARLY ASSOCIATED
WITH THE TOWN OF BIDA.

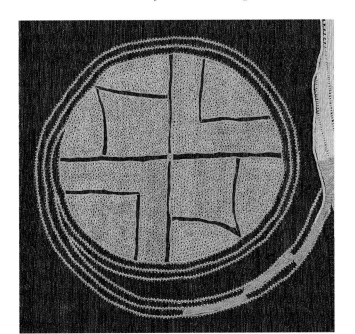

THE ELEGANT CROSSED CIRCLE
AND SPIRAL MOTIF IS FOUND
ON THE BACK AND THE RIGHT
CHEST OF THE ROBE, AS ON ALL
NORTHERN NIGERIAN GOWNS.

chapter 10

Printed and Dyed Textiles from Africa

Imported cotton cloth composed of dyed red warps and natural coloured cotton wefts. The combination of warps and wefts is used to create pairs of natural coloured cotton stripes. The cloth has been scrunched, tied and dyed using indigo. Probably from Senegal. 204.5 x 81.5 cm ($80^{1}/_{2}$ x 32 in). Donated by Charles A. Beving.

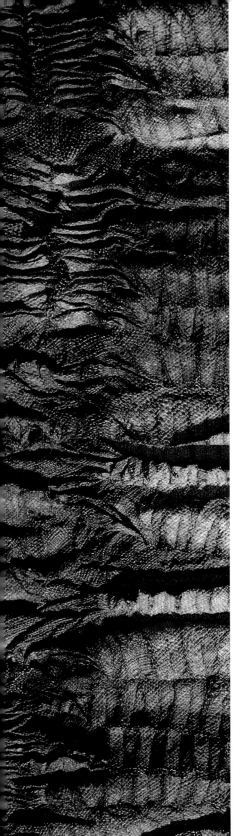

WOMAN'S CEREMONIAL SKIRT
Dida people, Coastal Cote d' Ivoire

This skirt is made of plaited raphia with
tied and stitched resist decoration in
yellow, brown and red-black.
60 × 40 cm (23 × 15 in)
Length including fringe: 93 cm (36²/₃ in)

THE BOLD COLOURS USED IN THIS DESIGN ARE ENRICHED BY
THE USE OF DEEP FOLDS. THIS CRINKLED TEXTURE
IS LEFT UNSMOOTHED, PERHAPS TO COMPLEMENT
THE CICATRICES (DECORATIVE SCARIFICATION) OF THE WEARER.

BARKCLOTHS WERE MADE IN LARGE NUMBERS IN UGANDA IN THE EARLIER PART OF
THE TWENTIETH CENTURY. THIS EXAMPLE IS PAINTED AND STAMPED TO CREATE A
BOLD PATTERN IN BLACK THAT LEAPS OUT FROM THE DEEP RED-BROWN OF THE BACKGROUND.

BOGOLANFINI ('MUD CLOTH')
Bamana people, Mali

This cotton mud cloth, probably worn as a women's wrap,
has been decorated using the mud-resist method, in
patterns based around circles, zigzags, triangles, crosses
and diamonds.
150 × 103 cm (59 × 40^1/$_2$ in)

THE BOGOLAN CLOTHS OF MALI ARE ESSENTIALLY PROTECTIVE IN NATURE. THEIR DISTINCTIVE DENSE PATTERNING, PAINTED IN NEGATIVE, IS BELIEVED TO ABSORB THREATENING SPIRITUAL FORCES.

THIS FINE EXAMPLE OF A MALI *BOGOLANFINI*, OR MUD CLOTH, GAINS DRAMATIC IMPACT FROM THE USE OF THE SAME WIDTH OF LINE THROUGH-OUT ALMOST THE ENTIRE DESIGN.

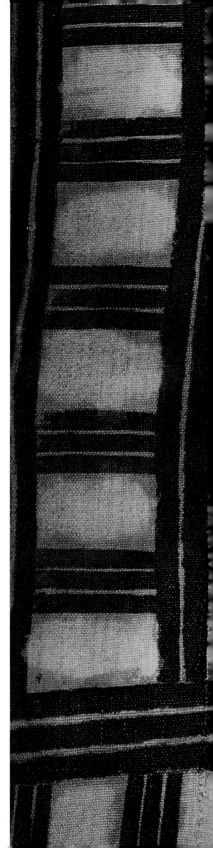

BOGOLANFINI ('MUD CLOTH')
Bamana people, Mali, mid-20th century

The cloth has been decorated using a resist
method producing weft rows of repeating
geometric patterns formed primarily using
circles, diamonds and stripes. Two edges
of the cloth are bordered.
136 × 104 cm (53 1/2 × 41 in)
Donated by Mrs Margaret Plass

MUCH FINER WORK IS EVIDENT IN THIS MUD
CLOTH, DATING FROM BEFORE WORLD WAR II,
THAN IN MODERN EXAMPLES. THIS DESIGN IS
ENLIVENED BY USING A BORDER PATTERN
ALONG TWO SIDES ONLY, CREATING A
POWERFUL ASSYMETRY.

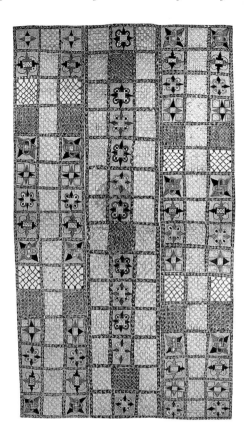

PAINTED CLOTH
Probably made by Hausa craftsmen for the
Asante people, Ghana

This cloth is divided into a grid, the lines of
which consist of painted triangles in red,
yellow, green and black.
348 × 200 cm (137 × 78 in)
Donated by Mrs Stevens

THIS COLOURFUL TALISMANIC CLOTH HAS A
STRONG ISLAMIC HERITAGE. ITS BOLD BUT
ORDERLY DESIGN INCLUDES MOTIFS INSPIRED
BY ARABIC CALLIGRAPHY – INTERPRETED IN A
STYLE THAT IS UNMISTAKABLY AFRICAN.

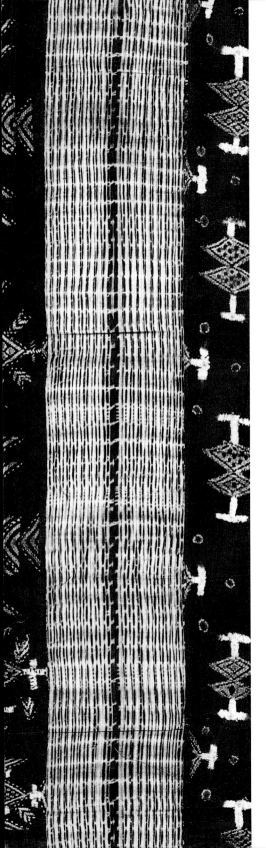
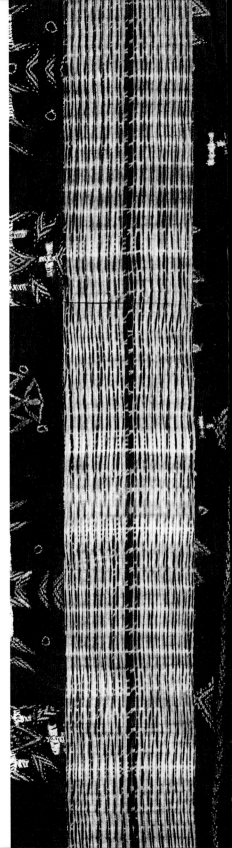

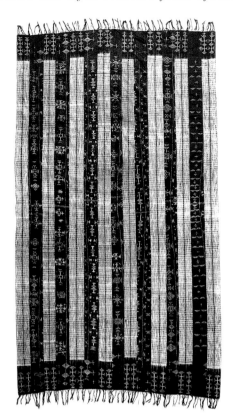

INDIGO-DYED CLOTH
St Louis, Senegal

The cloth has been decorated using the
stitch-resist technique
233 × 135 cm (91³/₄ × 53 in) without fringe
Donated by Charles A. Beving

THIS CLOTH HAS A LINEAR ARRANGEMENT OF
EMBROIDERED COTTON RESIST MOTIFS
ALTERNATING WITH SEWN, PLEATED AND
GATHERED RESIST BANDS. THE INTRICACY
OF THE FORMER (WHICH ARE PROBABLY
ISLAMIC-INSPIRED) IS BALANCED BY THE
SIMPLICITY OF THE LATTER.

ADIRE CLOTH
Yoruba people, Nigeria

Two patterns have been tied
and dyed with indigo, forming
alternating stripes
204 × 167 cm (80 × 65³/₄ in)

LARGE FLORAL MOTIFS ARE
CONTAINED WITHIN A TIGHTLY
ORGANIZED STRUCTURE OF
VERTICAL BANDS, IN A
MANNER REMINISCENT OF
THE PRINTED DESIGNS ON
IMPORTED MILL CLOTH.

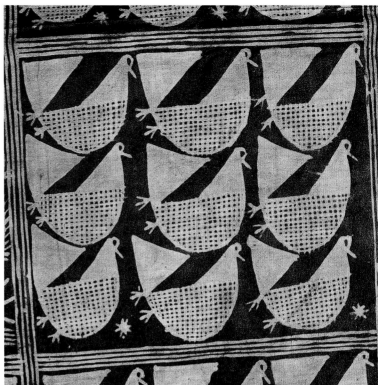
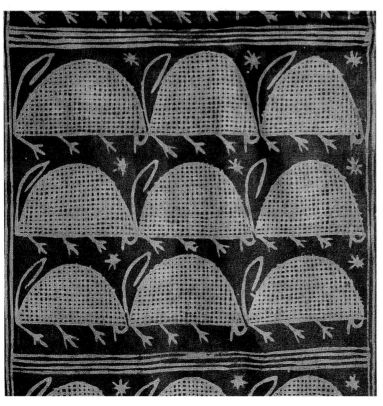

WOMAN'S WRAP
Yoruba people, Nigeria

An indigo-dyed *adire* cloth with hand-drawn design
190 × 173 cm (75 × 68 in)

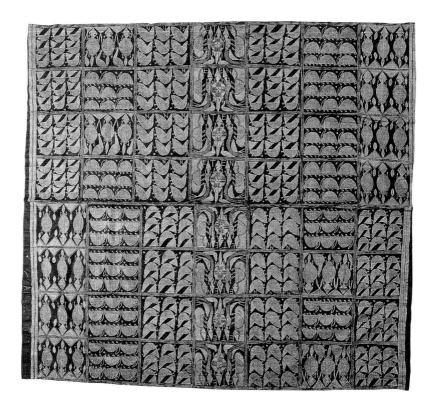

RATHER THAN BEING PURELY DECORATIVE, THE DESIGN MOTIFS ON AFRICAN
TEXTILES ARE OFTEN INTENDED TO PLAY A PROTECTIVE OR SYMBOLIC ROLE. THE
STYLIZED LIZARDS, BIRDS AND RODENTS ON THIS CLOTH HAVE MYTHIC OR MAGICAL
SIGNIFICANCE FOR THE YORUBA.

RESIST-SEWN CLOTH
Leopard society of Cross River,
south-eastern Nigeria

This cloth has been decorated using the stitch-
resist technique
242 × 177 cm (95 × 69½ in)

CLUTTERED WITH GEOMETRIC AND ANIMAL SHAPES, THIS
VIBRANT CHEQUERBOARD OF A DESIGN IS RICH WITH
SYMBOLISM. MANY OF ITS MOTIFS ARE THOUGHT TO
POSSESS SPECIAL POWERS.

WOMAN'S WRAP
Yorubaland, Nigeria

Indigo-dyed *adire* cloth with stencilled design.
173 × 194 cm (68 × 76 in)

THIS REPEAT PATTERN OF TOY-LIKE ELEPHANTS IS UNUSUAL IN ITS USE OF AN INSCRIPTION BENEATH EACH MOTIF.

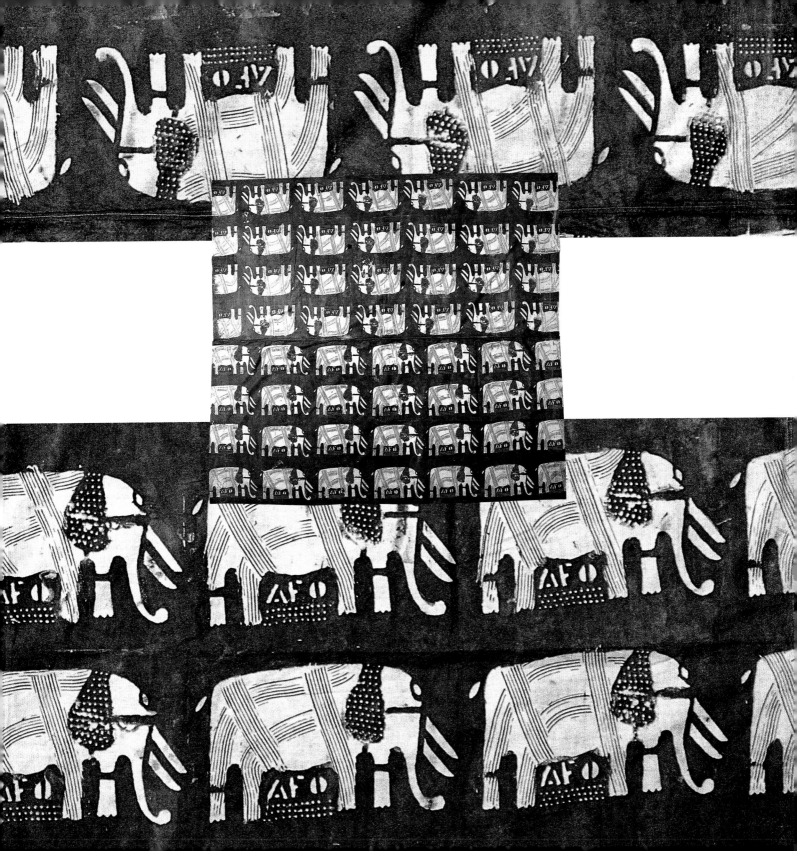

glossary

acrylics synthetic yarns. One of the best known acrylic fibres is acrilan – a substitute for wool.

adanudo one of the main cloths woven by the Ewe peoples for their own use. Often made of silk with WEFT-INLAY designs.

adinkra traditional fabric of Ghana, decorated with symbolic designs printed on by hand with stamps carved out of CALABASH gourds.

adire Yoruba word for RESIST dyeing with indigo.

adire alabere Yoruba stitched-resist dyeing technique.

adire eleko Yoruba technique whereby designs are painted or stencilled on to the cloth in a RESIST substance (starch paste) before dyeing it with INDIGO.

adiro oniko Yoruba dyeing technique using tied resists, usually of raphia.

agave *see* MAGUEY

alharini magenta WASTE SILK originally imported from Tunisia, later from Europe. Traded to Kano via trans-Saharan trade routes since the eleventh century.

Anaphe infracta a species of silkworm found wild in parts of Africa that is communal by nature and produces clusters of cocoons encased in a brown silk outer pod. Silk is obtained by de-gumming and spinning.

Anaphe moloneyi from the same genus as above. The silkworms form individual cocoons without an outer casing. The spun silk is used primarily for embroidery.

aniline dye derived from coal tar; developed commercially from the late 19th century.

aniline dyes name given to the early synthetic dyes, derived from coal tar, that revolutionized the dyeing industry after 1856.

animism The belief in the existence of individual spirits that inhabit natural objects and phenomena.

appliqué technique of stitching a supplementary piece of fabric on to a background cloth.

asante (also ashanti) ethnic group living in Ghana.

atlas silk satin fabric made in Syria.

backstrap loom simple portable loom traditionally used by women in various parts of the world since earliest times. The WARP is spread out on two rods, and tensioned between the weight of the woman's body at one end and a fixed point (on a post or tree) at the other. Also known as a hip loom, body-tensioned loom or stick loom.

bagh Punjabi woman's ceremonial shawl, where almost all the fabric is covered with embroidery; *see* also *PHULKARI*.

bakhnug one of three types of decorated shawl worn by women in the mountain areas south of Gabes, Tunisia.

barkcloth traditional cloth made by beating the inner bark from particular trees (in Africa, tropical fig trees).

batik Javanese method of resist-dyeing using wax.

Berber member of a large ethnic group who have inhabited most of North Africa for more than two Millennia.

binding ends warp threads that tie down the BROCADING thread at regular intervals.

blanket stitch an edging that usually covers the raw edges of blankets. It is used by the Lakai in a slanting version as a filling.

block printing decoration of a fabric by means of a carved wooden block dipped in dye.

body-tensioned loom simple portable loom, traditionally used by women in various parts of the world since earliest times. The warp is spread out on two rods and tensioned between the weight of the woman's body at one end and a fixed point (on a post or tree) at the other. Also known as a BACKSTRAP LOOM.

body-tensioned loom *see* BACKSTRAP LOOM

bogolanfini African mud-dyed ritual cloths of the Bamana people and other ethnic groups in Mali.

Bombyx mori domesticated silk moth that feeds primarily on mulberry leaves. It is reared extensively in Europe and China producing silk of outstanding quality and quantity. Its intensive domestication has resulted in it being rendered blind, flightless and without digestive organs.

brazilwood dyewood (*Haematoxylum brasiletto*) that gives purplish-red or deep tan shades.

brick stitch an alternating pattern of straight stitches set halfway between those of the previous row.

brocading method of producing designs with a supplementary WEFT. The thicker, contrasting thread skips over several warps at a time, standing out from the GROUND WEAVE (or background). *See* also SINGLE-FACED BROCADING, TWO-FACED BROCADING and DOUBLE-FACED BROCADING.

Bukhara couching technique where threads are held by small stitches of the same thread, staggered diagonally.

burqa a concealing cloak worn by Afghan women outside their homes. It hangs from a cap, with a fall covering the face and front bodice which can be pulled back in private when eating. A visor of drawn threadwork over the eyes enables the women to *see* without being seen.

calabash dried hollowed-out shell of a gourd from tropical trees of the same name; used for various purposes, including carrying water and other liquids.

calligraphy cloth Islamic-influenced cloth decorated with symbols based (often loosely) on Arabic calligraphy.

cassava starch derived from the tuberous root of tropical plants of the genus Manihot, which are also called cassava (or manioc).

ceiba tall, straight tree of the bombax family.

cellulose the main constituent of plant cell walls, used in the manufacture of rayon.

chain stitch a linear embroidery technique of connecting looped stitches. Each new stitch is drawn through the previous one, thus forming a chain.

chemise long shirt that forms the undergarment for most women's costumes; it is usually made of cotton or linen and often heavily embroidered on the parts that are seen.

chikan floral whitework embroidery, principally from Lucknow and Bengal.

chola backless bodice or blouse which forms part of the woman's costume in Gujarat, Rajasthan and Sindh.

chori Jath woman's full-skirted dress.

chyrpy embroidered cloak with vestigial sleeves, worn over the head by Turkmen women throughout Turkmen regions.

cochineal red dyestuff obtained from the bodies of insects.

cofradías religious brotherhoods with both church and civil responsibilities.

cola nut nut from the *Cola nitida* tree which, when crushed, yields a golden-brown dye; also chewed as a mild narcotic.

costumbre a custom or tradition (in the context of this book, especially in relation to COFRADIAS).

couching a method of sewing down a thick thread, bunch of threads, cord or gold with small stitches, at regular intervals, usually in a finer thread.

Counted threadwork an embroidery technique where motifs are worked by counting threads of the background fabric, as opposed to stitching freely.

coycuhe, coyuchi naturally brown cotton (*Gossypium mexicanum*) from the *Náhuatl coioichcatl*.

crochet a kind of chaining whereby the yarn is looped vertically and horizontally through two (or more) loops using a special needle with a small hook on the end.

cross stitch a COUNTED THREAD technique, where a

line of slanting stitches is worked along one direction and then crossed by another row in the opposite direction, forming a line of diagonal crosses.

cut-pile style of embroidery common among the Kuba people of the Congo. Similar to making candlewick, among the Kuba the technique consists of taking raphia threads through the surface of raphia fabric and trimming them off close to the surface with a sharp blade, which produces a velvety pile. Kuba cut-pile cloth is often referred to as *Kasai* velvet.

damask self-patterned satin-weave fabric in which the warps float over the wefts before being bound on the pattern areas, and under the wefts of the background, contrasting the two faces of satin; the fabric takes its name from the city of Damascus, where it first came to Western notice.

djiyak or *sheyraz* edging of needle- or card-weaving on Uzbek and Turkmen garments and other embroideries, worked directly on the cloth.

DMC Dolfus Mieg et Cie: French manufacturer of MERCERIZED cotton embroidery threads.

double-faced brocading BROCADED designs that are the same on both sides of the fabric.

draw loom special type of loom that increases the capacity for weaving figured fabrics. The loom is operated by the weaver and one or more assistants who 'draw up' the supplementary HEDDLES to form the pattern elements on a textile.

drawn threadwork an openwork technique whereby individual threads are removed from the cloth and the remaining threads are strengthened by binding, usually with other embroidery threads.

evil eye an envious and malevolent glance believed capable of serious injury, especially to children and anything precious.

famadihana second-burial ritual in Madagascar when the remains of the dead are disinterred and wrapped in a new silk shroud.

finial ornament set at the apex of a building or object.

flax the plant that provides the raw fibres for linen; the fibres are washed, beaten and hung or laid out in the sun to bleach.

float weave weave in which the weft passes over a number of warps to form a pattern.

floss silk raw silk threads unwound from the silkworm cocoon and sold in SKEINS; embroiderers combined the threads to the required thickness.

flying shuttle invented by John Kay in the early eighteenth century. A modified SHUTTLE BOAT runs along a track beneath the warp threads and is activated by the weaver pulling on a cord. This device increased output and allowed broader cloths to be made by a single weaver.

four-selvedge panel woven panel made to the exact size required, with SELVEDGES at top and bottom as well as at each side.

four-shaft treadle loom *see* TREADLE LOOM

fulled wool, or napped wool wool fabric that is felted by beating with water after it has been woven, as opposed to felt which is made of unwoven fibres.

gaghra full, gathered skirt.

gaiter a single piece of seamed cloth worn as a covering for the leg, from knee to ankle.

gauze loose-weave fabric in which pairs of warp threads twisted around each other are held in lace by the weft.

gauze-weaving selected warp threads are crossed and secured by the weft, creating an open, lace-like texture.

ginning removing the seeds from raw cotton with a machine called a gin.

goldwork embroidery using metallic threads.

ground weave the foundation fabric of interlaced warp and weft threads on which a design is worked.

gul-i-peron discs of decorated thread – incorporating shells, beads and other ornaments – stitched onto dresses and animal trappings, particularly by the Pashtun in Afghanistan.

gusset piece of material sewn into a garment, usually at the crotch or underarm.

heddle essential part of a loom, used to create the SHED openings through which the weft threads are passed.

hem stitch a decorative stitch (usually bordering a hem) made by drawing out several parallel threads and catching together the cross threads in uniform groups.

hemp tough-fibred Asian plant (*Cannabis sativa*) used to make yarn that is woven into cloth.

heremzi silk taffeta.

herringbone stitch an ornamental stitch characterized by an arrangement of rows in parallel lines, in which alternate rows slope in different directions.

hiladillo cochineal-dyed silk.

hip loom *see* BACKSTRAP LOOM

hizam belt used by men and women.

horizontal ground loom loom with warped threads mounted horizontally; warp beams are often pegged to the ground.

horizontal loom where the warp is stretched horizontally across vertical supports and the warp threads extend from front to back; as alternative threads are raised and lowered the weft is passed from side to side across the warp.

hram nfasiy wrap-around ceremonial cloth worn for the first time at marriage in El-Jem, Tunisia.

huipil (pronounced 'weepil') simple blouse or sleeveless tunic worn by Maya women of Central America, often BROCADED or embroidered on the upper part.

ikat RESIST-dyeing technique whereby sections of warp and/or weft yarn are bound before dyeing so that they are not coloured; this gives a broken edge to the woven patterns. This technique takes its name from the Indonesian word *mengikat*, which means to tie.

ikhdari 'green' fabric, and dress thereof; navy blue cotton or linen with green and red silk stripes, bordered by narrow yellow and red stripes, at the SELVEDGES; formerly woven in Mejdel and Bethlehem.

Ilgitsh a Lakai Uzbek wallhanging placed either side of the bedding pile; often in the shape of an envelope, but with a false flap.

indigo blue dye obtained from various plants of the genus *Indigofera*. If indigo is to 'take', exposure to the air is necessary (OXIDIZATION). Can also refer to the synthetic indigo dye.

interlacing an embroidery stitch based on a line of double herringbone, then interwoven several times with another thread. In Baluchi work the return thread is always of the same colour.

jap thread thread made by winding strips of paper covered in gold leaf around a silk core.

jaspe RESIST-dyed threads. Warp or weft threads are stretched out under tension and areas that are to remain white (or the original colour) are bound up with twine before dyeing. The binding is removed after the dye has been applied, thus revealing the jaspe designs.

jillayeh the finest coat or dress that the bride prepared for her trousseau.

jinneh-u-nar literally 'heaven-and-hell'; narrow white or blue fabric with green and red silk stripes at the SELVEDGE; formerly woven in El Mejdel, Palestine.

Job's tears tropical grass (*Coix lacryma-jobi*) from South East Asia, which bears hard, shiny seed-holding structures that are used as decorative beads.

kamis woman's dress in contemporary Ethiopia, the name deriving from the French 'chemise'.

kantha quilted embroidery of Bengal and north-east India.

kente ceremonial strip-woven cloth of the Asante people of Ghana. Commonly used as a general term for Asante silk textiles.

kermes an insect-based natural dye which gives shades of red, orange and yellow.

kesdi embroidery stitch, typical of Turkmen work; it is a version of double CHAIN STITCH, worked extremely closely.

khaddar coarse cotton cloth, formerly hand-woven; *see* also *PHULKARI*.

khirqah headveil made from two widths of fabric.

kohl a black powder of antimony or lead sulphide used as eye make-up and also believed to offer protection from both flies and evil spirits.

kilim flat woven carpet.

Kuba a confederation of peoples centred around the Kasai river area in the Congo, Africa.

lafun CASSAVA or corn starch used by the Yoruba people as a resist medium in the making of hand-drawn or stencilled ADIRE cloths.

lamba generic name for cloth in Madagascar.

lamba akotofahana silk cloth of complex pattern used by the nobility of the nineteenth-century kingdom of Imerina in Madagascar.

lamd honorific cape worn by high-ranking secular and religious officials in Ethiopia.

lozenge diamond-shaped design.

loznitsa a trellis vine ornamentation.

lurex synthetic metal thread.

lusheng pipes traditional bamboo reed pipes played by the Miao.

Maghreb (meaning 'the West' in Arabic) North Africa, usually taken as excluding Egypt.

maguey tropical plants of the Agave family; can also refer to the fibres extracted from their fleshy leaves.

malak literally 'royal' fabric; fabric with silk warp stripes and rows of rosettes, formerly woven in Bethlehem; *thob malak* or *malakeh* – the best dress contributed by the groom to the trousseau; commissioned from professional embroiderers mainly in the Bethlehem area.

mercerized or perle cotton spun cotton threads manufactured with a sheen imitating silk.

metal threadwork various embroidery techniques using threads of metal instead of fibre.

mochi the work made by male professional embroiderers in Gujarat, India.

mohr SHI'A prayer stone of terracotta from Kerbela, Iraq. These should be brought back by pilgrims and not traded.

mohr posh embroidered prayer cloth made by women or girls in which to wrap the MOHR. This cloth should be laid on a prayer mat and the *mohr* placed on it where the pattern indicates.

mordant a metallic salt that reacts chemically with a dyestuff to fix the dye so that it is permanent.

mujahedin Islamic guerrilla fighters.

okbash pair of bags, woven or felted, used to protect the ends of yurt poles during transport.

openwork *see* DRAWN and PULLED THREADWORK.

outline stitch *see* STEM STITCH.

oxidization to combine with oxygen.

papercuts pieces of paper with patterns drawn on them (often stitched through to create the design and left on the finished garment).

pattern darning COUNTED-THREAD technique worked in a RUNNING STITCH, used for geometric designs.

perraje shawl or wrap.

phulkari 'flower-work' embroideries of floss silk on KHADDAR cotton, in geometric patterns worked from the reverse; principally from Punjab and used mainly as shawls.

phyllomorphic in a shape or form that represents plants.

pudo long pocket extending from waist to hem, with an inverted V at the waist; typical of Baluchi women's dress.

pulled threadwork an open technique created by teasing threads of the GROUND fabric apart (but not removing them) and binding the remaining threads together.

puttees embroidered bands to wind round the lower leg of trousers.

quechquemitl woman's closed shoulder-cape of pre-Conquest origin (Náhuatl term).

quetzal Central American bird (*Pharomachrus mocinno*) known for its brilliant colours, especially on the male's tail feathers; now an endangered species.

quilting process of stitching together several layers of fabric to create a warm or protective cloth.

raised where the BROCADING thread is lifted slightly

between the BINDING ENDS, by a flick of the finger, to give an uncut pile effect.

ramie   woody Asian plant (*Boehmeria nivea*) of the nettle family, from which yarn is made for weaving into cloth, cord, etc; the word is also used to mean the cloth itself.

randa   decorative stitch worked in a variety of colours to join two panels SELVEDGE to selvedge; featured on skirts, *HUIPILS* and various cloths.

raw silk   silk retaining its natural gum that resists dye. Usually de-gummed by heating in an alkaline solution.

rebozo   woman's rectangular shawl.

resist   a substance (such as starch or wax) or technique (such as tying or stitching) employed to prevent dye from penetrating certain areas of a fabric, in order to create a design in contrasting colours. *See* WAX RESIST.

rhomboid   LOZENGE-shaped design or parallelogram.

rick rack   machine-woven braid in a meander or zigzag pattern, used to decorate garments.

rouleau   coil or roll made of ribbon or strips of fabric.

running stitch   flat stitch that involves taking the needle and thread through the cloth at regularly spaced intervals.

sarape   blanket, often with an opening for the head.

sateen   woven fabric with a glossy, satin-like finish.

satin stitch   long, straight embroidery stitch. Each stitch is worked parallel to and touching the next, usually across the shape of a particular design motif.

selvedge (or selvage)   side edge of a fabric, where the WEFT returns – the non-fraying edge of a piece of cloth.

servilleta   cloth, often used for ceremonial purposes or to cover food.

shafts   the slat of wood on a treadle loom that support the HEDDLES.

shalwar   full, gathered trousers, part of the shalwar-kameez trouser and tunic costume worn in Pakistan by both men and women.

shalwar-kameez   outfit of baggy trousers tied at the waist and loose straight shirt worn by men, women and children in Pakistan, and now in many parts of Central Asia.

shamma   toga-like shawl worn by men and women throughout Ethiopia.

shed   on a loom, the opening made between two layers of warp threads, through which the shuttle is passed.

shed stick   sticks placed between warp elements to allow the weft to be passed through to form patterns.

Shi'a or Shi'ite   one of the two main branches of Islam; believers follow Ali, son-in-law of Mohammed, and his direct descendants.

shisha   mirror glass, broken and cut into small pieces (usually circles) and used as a decorative feature of embroidery.

shuttle boat   device used to pass thread through the SHED.

silk   natural filament obtained from the cocoons of silkworms.

single-faced brocading   BROCADING in which the design appears on the face of the fabric only.

smocking   gathering material into tight pleats, which are then stitched together.

sobrehuipil   larger *huipil* of Central America, worn as an overgarment on top of the everyday one, especially on ceremonial occasions.

soof   geometric counted-thread embroidery of Sindh and Kutch.

soumak   decorative weaving technique whereby wefts are wrapped around warps (instead of being interlaced with them), which produces a surface texture similar to CHAIN STITCH.

spindle   implement for drawing out and twisting fibres into thread. In rural Mexico, yarn is still spun in pre-Conquest fashion: the spinner rapidly rotates the spindle, which has a wooden shaft weighted with a round WHORL.

sprang   a two-ended method of interlinking a set of lengthways threads

stem stitch   flat embroidery stitch. The needle is brought out to the left of the stitches that proceed upwards. When the needle is brought out to the right, the stitch is termed OUTLINE.

stepped fret   geometric design, usually repeated to

form a decorative band, combining steps with a central scroll or hook. Much used in pre-conquest Mexico, it may have been a stylization of the serpent.

stick loom *see* BACKSTRAP LOOM.

stocking stitch (also known as stockinette stitch) the most basic knitted fabric; every stitch (as seen from the right side) is a knit stitch.

strip-woven made up by sewing narrow strips of woven cloth together, SELVEDGE to selvedge; strip-woven fabrics are found throughout West Africa.

substantive dye one that does not require a MORDANT to render it permanent.

Sunni the branch of Islam that accepts the authority of all-elected caliphs (heads of states) as civil and religious leaders and successors of Mohammed.

supplementary weft a contrasting (and sometimes thicker) ornamental thread added to the GROUND yarn to form a woven design.

sura chapter or verse from the Koran.

suzani Uzbek domestic cloth made of strips of cotton fabric, or occasionally silk, embroidered by several women and then joined together; decoration is usually floral but can be astral, and styles are attributed to different towns in Uzbekistan.

swastika equal-armed cross with the ends of each arm extended at opposite right angles.

swidden land cleared for cultivation by slashing and burning the existing vegetation.

tablet loom a small simple hand-held loom used to make belts or other narrow pieces of cloth. The warps are threaded through small tablets or cards pierced with holes and tensioned at either end. The tablets are rotated, either in groups or singly, to form different weaving SHEDS for the wefts to pass through.

Taliban Afghan fundamentalist Islamic fighters, who gradually took over power in Afghanistan from 1994 to 2001 when they were ousted by a US-led military operation.

tanshifa Algerian woman's embroidered linen shawl; reserved for special occasions.

tapestry weaving technique for creating designs or pictures in cloth. Weft threads move across selected areas, not from SELVEDGE to selvedge.

taqsireh jacket of broadcloth (earlier) or velvet (later).

terzidhes male tailors from Greece.

thob dress

tie-and-dye (or tie-dye) a widely used RESIST technique that involves enclosing portions of a fabric within tightly drawn thread ties to prevent them from taking up the dye; it results in (usually circular) patterns that stand out in the original colour of the cloth against a dyed background.

tishrimeh (also *tishrifeh*) zigzag appliqué used for framing and edging.

traje traditional costume of the Maya in Central America.

treadle loom sturdy foot-operated floor loom with SHAFTS for raising and lowering the threads. The shafts are attached to treadles, which increases the speed of weaving, compared with the BACKSTRAP LOOM.

trousseau The possessions, such as clothing and linens, that a bride assembles for her marriage.

twill fabric/weave each passage of the weft through the warps goes over two, under one, over two, under one. In the next passage, the same sequence is repeated but staggered, to produce diagonal lines on the face of the cloth. A diagonal, chevron or diamond pattern can be produced by adjusting the sequencing.

two-faced brocading technique whereby the design on the face of a fabric appears in negative on the reverse; work produced by this technique.

tzute (pronounced 'shoot') Maya term used for a variety of rectangular cloths, such as head-cloths, *SERVILLETA* and all purpose carrying cloths.

ukura term for pictorial INDIGO-dyed stitch-RESIST cloths made in northern Igboland for such organizations as the Leopard Society of the Cross River area of south-east Nigeria.

vertical loom an upright loom where the warp is stretched vertically. In the Balkans, it is used for carpet making, usually done by women on a loom in their own house.

warp threads that stretch lengthways in a fabric.
warp-faced with the warp threads predominating over the weft (which is almost obscured).
waste silk by-product of silk processing; obtained from broken cocoons which cannot be reeled (wound), the short threads are spun in a manner similar to cotton and wool.
wax resist design technique that involves preventing certain areas of a fabric from accepting the dye. The design is drawn in a dye-resistant substance known as a RESIST (such as a wax or paste), or worked in stitches, so that after the dyeing it is still the same colour and stands out against the dyed areas.
weft the thread that is passed from SELVEDGE to selvedge in a woven structure.
weft transverse threads that interlace with the warp.
weft-faced term describing a fabric in which the weft completely covers the warp.
weft-float supplementary weft that is 'floated' across a warp-faced textile to form patterns.
weft-inlay supplementary discontinuous weft forming blocks of inlay pattern.
whitework embroidery in white thread on white fabric.
whorl disk of clay or wood on the lower part of the SPINDLE.

Yoke A piece of a garment that is closely fitted, either around the neck and shoulders or at the hips, and from which an unfitted or gathered part of the garment is hung.
Yoruba large ethnic group living in south-west Nigeria.
yurt circular tent made of a collapsible framework covered with felt or skins.

zoomorphic in a shape or form that represents animals.

picture credits

selected reading

General

Anawalt, P.R., *The Worldwide History of Dress*, Thames and Hudson, 2007

Balfour- Paul, J., *Indigo: Egyptian Mummies to Blue Jeans*, British Museum Press, 1998, rev. edn 2011

Burnam, D.K., *Warp and Weft: A Textile Terminology*, Royal Ontario Museum, 1980

Eicher, J.B. (ed.), *Berg Encyclopedia of World Dress and Fashion*, Berg Publishers, 2010

Gillow, J., and B. Sentence, *World Textiles: A Visual Guide to Traditional Techniques*, Thames and Hudson, 1999

Harris, J. (ed.), *5000 Years of Textiles*, British Museum Press, 1993, rev. edn 2010

Hecht, A., *The Art of the Loom: Weaving, Spinning and Dyeing across the World*, British Museum Press, 1989

Paine, S., *Embroidered Textiles: A World Guide to Traditional Patterns*, Thames and Hudson, 2008

Seiler-Baldinger, A., *Textiles: a Classification of Techniques*, Crawford House Press, 1994

Textiles from the Balkans

Gjergil, A., *Albanian Folk Costumes* (*Veshje popullore shqiptare*), 3 vols. Instituti i Kulturës Popullore, Tirenë. Vol. 1, 1999; vol. 2 by M. Tira, A. Dojaka and Y. Selimi, 2001; vol. 3, 2004

Hatizimichali, A., *The Greek Folklore Costume*, vols 1 and 2, Benaki Museum, 1977

Kwasnik, E. (ed.), *British and Bulgarian Ethnology*, National Museums and Galleries on Merseyside, 1992

Macdermott, M., *Bulgarian Folk Customs*, Jessica Kingsley Publishers, 1998

Pantelic, N., *Traditional Arts and Crafts in Yugoslavia*, Jugoslovenska Revija, 1984

Embroidery from Palestine

Kawar, W., *Threads of Identity: Preserving Palestinian Costume and Heritage*, Rimal Publications, 2010

Rajab, J., *Palestinian Costume*, Keegan Paul, 1989

Skinner, M., *Palestinian Embroidery Motifs: a treasury of stitches 1850–1950*, Melisende Publishing/Rimal Publications, 2007

Weir, S., *Palestinian Costume*, British Museum Press, 1989, repr. 1990, pbk edn 1994

Embroidery from Afghanistan

Dupaigne, B., *Afghan Embroidery*, Ferozsons PVT Ltd, 1993

Fitz Gibbon, K., and A. Hale, *Uzbek Embroidery in the Nomadic Tradition*, Minneapolis Institute of Arts, 2007

Gillow, J., *Textiles from the Islamic World*, Thames and Hudson, 2010

Harvey, J., *Traditional Textiles from Central Asia*, Thames and Hudson, 1997

Paine, S., *Amulets: A World of Secret Powers, Charms and Magic*, Thames and Hudson, 2004

Embroidery from India and Pakistan

Askari, N., and R. Crill, *Colours of the Indus*, Victoria and Albert Museum/Merrell Holberton, 1997

Crill, R., *Indian Embroidery*, Victoria and Albert Museum, 1999

Gillow, J., and N. Barnard, *Indian Textiles*, Thames and Hudson, 2008

Kumar, R., *Costume and Textiles of Royal India*, Christie Books, 1999

Morrell, A., *The Techniques of Indian Embroidery*, B.T. Batsford, 1994

Miao Textiles from China

Cultural Palace of Nationalities, *Clothing and Ornaments of China's Miao People*, Nationality Press, 1985

O'Connor, D., *Miao Costumes from Guizhou Province*, James Hockey Gallery, West Surrey College of Art and Design, 1994

Smith, R., *Miao Embroidery from South West China: Textiles from the Gina Corrigan Collection*, Occidor Ltd, 2005

Smith, R., *Minority Textile Techniques: Costumes from South West China*, Occidor Ltd, 2007

Writing with Thread: Traditional Textiles of Southwest Chinese Minorities, University of Hawai'i Art Gallery, 2009

Textiles from Guatemala

Deuss, K., *Indian Costumes from Guatemala*, Paladin Graphics, 1981

Hecht, A., *Guatemalan Textiles in the British Museum*, Occasional Paper 134, British Museum Press, 2001

Pettersen, C.L., *The Maya of Guatemala: Life and Dress*, University of Washington Press, 1977

Rowe, A.P., *A Century of Change in Guatemalan Textiles*, University of Washington Press, 1981

Schevill, M.B., *Maya Textiles of Guatemala: The Gustavus A. Eisen Collection, 1902*, University of Texas Press, 1993

Textiles from Mexico

Anawalt, P.R., *Indian Clothing Before Cortés: Mesoamerican Costumes from the Codices*, University of Oklahoma Press, 1981

Cordry, D.B. and D.M., *Mexican Indian Costumes*, University of Texas Press, 1968

Johnson, I.W., *Design Motifs on Mexican Indian Textiles*, 2 vols, Akademische Druck und Verlagsanstalt, 1976

Morris, W.F., *Living Maya*, Harry N. Abrahams Inc., 1987

Sayer, C., *Mexican Textiles*, British Museum Press, 1998

Textiles from the Andes

Paul, A., *Paracas Ritual Attire: Symbols of Authority in Ancient Peru*, University of Oklahoma Press, 1990

Rowe, A.P., *Warp-Patterned Weaves of the Andes*, Textile Museum, Washington D.C., 1977

Rowe, A.P., *Costumes and Featherwork of the Lords of Chimor: Textiles from Peru's North Coast*, Textile Museum, Washington D.C., 1984

Stone-Miller, R., *To Weave for the Sun: Ancient Andean Textiles*, Thames and Hudson, 1994

Silk in Africa

Clarke, D., *The Art of African Textiles*, Thunder Bay Press, 1997

La Gamma, A., and C. Guintini, *The Essential Art of African Textiles: Design without End*, Metropolitan Museum of Art, 2008

Lamb, V., *West African Weaving*, Gerald Duckworth & Co., 1975

Picton, J., and J. Mack, *African Textiles*, British Museum Press, 1989

Spring, C., and J. Hudson, *North African Textiles*, British Museum Press, 1995

Printed and Dyed Textiles from Africa

Gillow, J., *African Textiles: Colour and creativity across a continent*, Thames and Hudson, 2003

Picton, J., *The Art of African Textiles*, Barbican Art Gallery, 1995

Polakoff, C., *African Textiles and Dyeing Techniques*, Routledge, 1982

Relph, M., and R. Irwin, *African Wax Print: A Textile Journey*, Words and Pixels, 2010

Sandberg, G., *Indigo Textiles: Techniques and History*, A&C Black, 1989

museum accession numbers

index